TRIBES OF LEGEND
FANTASY, MYTHS, MAGIC & MAYHEM
GAMING & MODELLING IN THE
WORLD OF GREEK GODS & LEGENDS

Concept & Games Design: Jake Thornton

Games Development: Jake Thornton, Matthew Fletcher & Ronnie Shilton.

Painting Guides: Kevin Dallimore & Jez Griffin.

Additional Material: Martin Buck, Matthew Fletcher & Kevin Dallimore.

Editing: Martin Buck & Keith Pinfold.

Playtesting: Richard Baker, Andy Clark, Kevin Dallimore, Matthew Fletcher, Richard Jeffery, Bob Parnham, Geoff Savory, Ronnie Shilton,

BOOK PRODUCTION

Cover Art. The Hydra and the Golden Fleece (front); Perseus and Medusa (back) © 2011 Howard David Johnson.

Internal Art. The Greek Heroes (page 5); In the wake of Poisedon (page 24); King Leonidas of Sparta (page 40); Achilles Triumphant (page 50); Bellerophon and Pegasus (page 66) © 2011 Howard David Johnson. *http://www.howarddavidjohnson.com/*

Diagram & Concept Art: Martin Buck.

Layout & Graphic Design: Kevin Dallimore.

Photography: Kevin Dallimore.

Below. Centaurs and Satyrs at war!

MINIATURES & SCENERY

All miniatures produced by:
Foundry Miniatures Ltd.

Visit www.wargamesfoundry.com

Miniature Painting: Matthew Fletcher, Jez Griffin, Martin Buck & Kevin Dallimore.

Miniatures from the collections of: Foundry, Matthew Fletcher & Kevin Dallimore.

Scenery Modelling: Matthew Fletcher, Kevin Dallimore and resin buildings by Monolith Design

Scenery from the collections of: Foundry, Matthew Fletcher, & Kevin Dallimore.

First published in Great Britain in 2011

By Foundry Publications, 24-34 St Mark's Street, NG3 1DE, United Kingdom. Tel 0115 841 3000.

ISBN 10 1-901543-28-5

ISBN 13 978-1-901543-28-5

CONTENTS

Ares.

CONTENTS

INTRODUCTION

There are many writings about ancient cultures lurking in the dusty books of academia, but few capture the imagination like the legends and myths of the ancient Greeks where heroes and monsters live or die in struggles for survival, honour and glory – all under the watchful gaze of their meddlesome gods.

These tales not only evoke images of warriors in gleaming bronze armour and beautiful women dressed in flowing white robes, but relate many wondrous stories of heroism and adventure, death and glory; the noble sacrifice of the 300 Spartans, the famous deception of the wooden horse and the voyage of Jason and the Argonauts to name but three.

This book contains not one, but three separate games set in this ancient world of myth, magic and monsters, ranging from full scale battles to a game for a single hero having

to overcome all of the obstacles that mortals and gods in their whim and wisdom devise.

However, this book is much more than a collection of games for it also includes guides for building terrain on your tabletop and a series of step-by-step instructions on how to paint the models you might want to play with - the photographs in this book show the models at their best, in their natural habitat: heroes and monsters locked in honourable combat.

So what will be your first foray into this ancient realm? Are you a lone hero or a leader of armies?

Decide, and then summon your courage, offer your prayer and, whichever game you play, may the gods smile on you.

Jake Thornton

Below. Harpies ambush a band of Centaur Colts. The youngsters of the Centaur tribes are boisterous and usually spoiling for a fight.

TRIBES OF LEGEND

In the earliest period of the Heroic Age of Ancient Greece, tribes of Centaurs and Satyrs vied with the warriors of fledgling city-states, and heroes and Gods roamed the battlefields at will. The Greeks thought of this age as a part of their history and considered it as real as any other time. Before dismissing it as fantasy, remember that the Trojan War was also once thought to have been purely myth and now archaeology has shown that conflict to be based in fact; it seems all mythical tales have their roots hidden in reality…

GAME OVERVIEW

Each player takes the part of a heroic leader of his chosen tribe and will lead an army against the forces of another tribe, commanded by a second player. Armies at this time were fairly small, so the objectives that appear in each game are important to achieving victory, even though they may only be livestock or a sacred spring.

After the objectives are placed and the armies are arrayed for battle, the game continues in a series of turns. In each turn both players will be able to "activate" all of their units. This is done one at a time, with players alternating. As it activates, a unit moves, shoots and fights as it needs to. This gives the battle much more of an interactive ebb and flow than systems where one player acts with his whole army at a time.

The combat system is fairly brutal, with units being removed completely when they are broken or lose half of their number. There is also a big difference in survivability between different unit types. For example, heavily armoured, sturdy Hoplite units last much longer than lightly armed, skirmishing Peltasts. The skill lies in attacking the enemy at their weak points.

As soon as one army has lost half its strength (measured in *Army Points*) it loses the battle.

WHAT YOU NEED TO PLAY

- An army of mythical Greek models for each player. Models can be based individually or in groups. Each unit of models needs a distinct leader model or base. See below for the way that units are deployed in the game.

- A table to fight the battle on. Six foot by four foot is an ideal size.

- A selection of scenery elements to make the battles more interesting. See below for the different types you can choose from.

- *Hand of the Gods* cards (included at the end of these rules).

- Eight to twelve six-sided dice per player.

- If your models are on multiple bases, you will need some small round plastic tokens to keep track of wounds.

- Optionally, you may want some counters, glass beads or similar to remind you which units have been activated that turn. Make sure they are distinct from any markers you use for wounds, to avoid confusion.

MEASURING

If you want to play these rules using a metric tape measure, multiply the distance given in inches by two to give the number of centimetres to be moved. To restrict all bloodshed to the tabletop, it is highly recommended that all players agree before the battle commences which measuring system is to be used!

Below. Three units of Centaurs prepare to attack. Commonly one unit or other charges off into the fray before the rest of the army is ready. Skilful commanders learn to adapt as the battle flows, making best use of these unpredicted assaults.

Above. The oldest and largest of the Centaurs fight in bands known as Destriers. They are considerably tougher and more dangerous than the bulk of the tribe and are no more controllable.

CHOOSING YOUR TRIBE

There are a number of tribes to choose from, each possessing strengths and weaknesses. Rather than worry about which is the most competitive, your best bet is to read the background, have a look at all the models and then pick the tribe that appeals to you most. Whether you have chosen an army because it looks impressive, because it fits your tactical style, or simply because you find the idea of a mob of drunks amusing (like I do) the army that you find most engaging is the one you will play longest and get the most enjoyment from.

When you have made your decision, you need to organise your forces for the battle. You have a total of fifteen *Army Points* to spend on the units in your army, chosen from the lists below. You can end up spending less than this if the unit costs do not quite add up right, but you cannot spend more. In addition, each army must bring along two camp follower pieces that will serve as objectives for the enemy. The camp followers cost no *Army Points* and are a great little modelling project to go to town on. They have no interaction with the rest of the game models so it does not matter how they are based, but it is best to keep them on bases no bigger than a CD. Camp follower bases can include tents and campfires, herds of animals and herders/shepherds, civilians, priests sacrificing goats, sacred springs and so on.

Have a look at the civilian model ranges and see what you can think up. Really good looking objectives will make a big difference to the whole feel of the game, so it is worth putting in a little extra modelling work here.

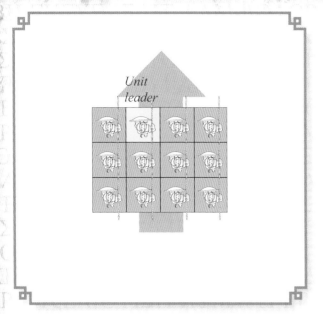

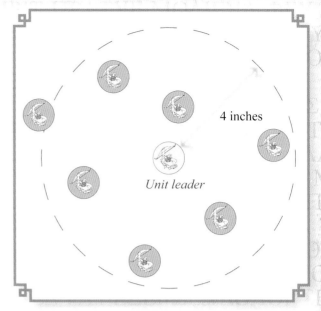

Above. Formed Unit. The ranks are four models wide. Place the unit leader in the front rank in either of the centre-most positions.

Above. Loose Unit. Models in loose units must set up and remain within 4 inches of their unit leader at all times.

FORMING YOUR ARMY

Once you have decided on your tribe and worked out the units in your army, you need to put it all together. As noted earlier, it does not matter how your models are based, but for multiple model bases you will need to find some tokens to mark casualties. The important thing is that each unit has an easily distinguishable leader model. The leader is used as the point from which, and to which, you will measure all ranges, so it is a good idea to have an easily identifiable leader model to avoid arguments. If there is any doubt, then point out to your opponent which model is the leader of each unit at the start of the game.

Formed Units

Properly drilled troops retain a fixed formation throughout a battle. The models are placed with bases touching in ranks and files. The ranks are four models wide, so a

sixteen strong unit would be four wide and four deep. Place the unit leader in the front rank in either of the centremost positions.

Formed units have four sides: front, left flank, right flank and rear. They also have four arcs around them, dividing the area around the unit into four equal ninety-degree segments. This is important when shooting and moving to contact the enemy, and when being the subject of these attacks.

Loose Units

Models in loose units do not have to form up touching other models in their unit. All that is required of them is that they set up and remain within four inches of their unit leader at all times.

Loose units can move and shoot in any direction. They have no flank or rear sides, or arcs.

Below. Formed units have four sides: front, left flank, right flank and rear.

Below. Loose units can move and shoot in any direction. They have no flanks or rear sides or arcs.

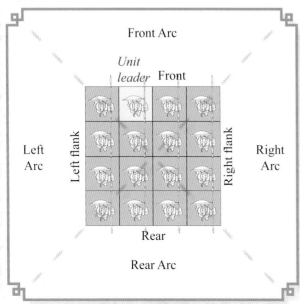

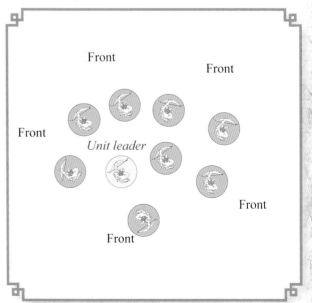

Above. Centaurs attack a band of Harpies. The Centaurs' strength and weakness is the same thing; drink!

TRIBAL LISTINGS

There are five tribes to choose from: City-states, Hillmen, Amazons, Centaurs and Satyrs. The different tribes are described below in a standard format listing the following information:

Unit Name: the name for this type of unit.

Cost: the number of *Army Points* it costs to include a single unit of this type in your army.

Type: whether the unit fights in a loose or formed formation.

Models: how many models there are in the unit at the start of the game.

Movement Rate: how fast the unit moves (in inches).

Attack: the attack skill of the unit's troops.

Defence: the defence skill of the unit's troops.

Special Rules: any special rules that apply to the unit. Special rules are additions and exceptions to the normal rules. They only apply to a few troops and so are only listed where appropriate. If nothing is listed here then the unit has no special rules.

Below. Pan plays wildly on his pipes to drive the Satyrs into a fighting frenzy!

CITY-STATES

Perhaps Village-states would be more accurate at this point in time; Town-states at best. Still, they are the shiniest beacons of civilisation in this early stage of Greek history. Unlike every other army, their core troops are rigorously drilled in formations and manoeuvres. Most of the other tribes consider this to be effeminate posturing rather than the stuff of real warriors. However, on the battlefield it can be quite formidable.

Unit Name	Cost	Type	Models	Movement Rate	Attack	Defence	Special Rules
Chosen Band	6	Formed	12	6	4	4	Unflinching
Hoplites	4	Formed	16	6	5	4	
Peltasts	1	Loose	8	10	6	6	Shoot (6)

CHOSEN BAND

Once a warrior has proven himself in many battles, when his courage and skill are utterly unquestioned, then he can be considered for the Chosen Band. These elite warriors are all tried and tested veterans who have seen the horrors of war and were not impressed. They are generally used as a rock to anchor a battle line, as they will fight regardless of the odds and die where they stand rather than dishonour themselves by retreat.

HOPLITES

The citizen soldiers of the City-states are well equipped and rigorously drilled. It is their duty to provide themselves with arms and armour and train hard so that they can better defend their state with their lives. Hoplites are armed with a round shield, called a *hoplon*, which covers them from neck to knee. With a helmet, cuirass and greaves as well, and fighting in a close formation, they offer few gaps for enemy weapons to strike anything except armour.

PELTASTS

The light troops of a City-state's army are Peltasts, so called for the distinctively shaped *pelta* shield they sometimes carry. They use a variety of missile weapons in battle including javelins, slings and occasionally bows. Regardless of their armament they perform the same function; to keep the enemy riff-raff from getting in the way of the citizenry while they get on with the business of winning the battle. Peltasts are a match for most enemy light troops, but have trouble with anything heavier.

Special Rules

The following special rules apply to troops in this tribe.

Unflinching: units with this ability do not retreat from enemy shooting and will fight to the last man (or Amazon, or Centaur…) regardless of casualties, but their stubborn unwillingness to give ground as a unit is not always the best plan for the individual. If their opponent rolls enough to break them in melee then the unit remains in play. However, a unit that should have broken loses an additional model instead to represent the ones who are killed grimly holding their ground rather than sensibly falling back. *Unflinching* units are not removed when they get to half strength as others are. Instead they continue to move and fight as normal until they are wiped out completely.

Shoot (x): most troops do not have any ability to damage the enemy at a distance. If a unit is equipped with bows, slings, javelins or other missile weapons then they will have the *Shoot* ability. The number in brackets is the attack value of the unit's shooting attacks.

Below. Hoplites, the citizen soldiers of the City-states, are well equipped and rigorously drilled.

HILLMEN

Above. The most common units in a tribe of Hillmen are the Tribesmen themselves.

HILLMEN

During this period in Greece, the hills are alive with tribes that are generally considered uncivilised and dangerous. Many armies include them as mercenaries and their fighting prowess is legendary. With no written language for the majority of hill peoples, their history is told only in the annals of those who suffer their raids and attempt to conquer their lands. It is not surprising that we have such a polarised view of them.

Hillmen armies are swarms of dangerous warriors, big on attack and somewhat lacking in defence. They are ferocious in assault, but lack resilience. The challenge of fielding a successful tribe lies in bringing this ferocity to bear effectively.

Unit Name	Cost	Type	Models	Movement Rate	Attack	Defence	Special Rules
Avengers	3	Loose	8	8	3	5	
Tribesmen	2	Loose	12	8	4	6	
Youngsters	2	Loose	12	10	5	6	Shoot (6)

AVENGERS

Of those that leave the tribe to seek adventure as mercenaries, few return. Most are lost on some far-off battlefield, fighting for a cause they do not understand and a leader that does not understand them. The few that do return are given a great deal of respect by the rest of the tribe and quickly find themselves in positions of prominence. When the tribe fights, it is these Avengers that form the toughest of their units, their skills and experience making them formidable fighters.

TRIBESMEN

The most common units in a tribe of Hillmen are the Tribesmen themselves. In time of peril, any able-bodied male will take up arms in defence of the tribe. Anyone who is old enough, but not yet renowned enough to be classed as an Avenger, will count as a Tribesman. Most Tribesmen carry spears and knives or daggers but have little in the way of armour except, perhaps, a leather cloak.

What defence they have is mainly due to their nimbleness and stubborn resilience to wounds.

YOUNGSTERS

The children of the hill tribes learn to fight at an early age, so when the tribe is threatened they are expected to join in the defence. They are not expected to stand in the main line of battle as they lack the experience. Instead they fight on the edges of the conflict, shooting at distant enemies and gaining vital experience so that they can join their elders when the next danger comes.

Special Rules

The following special rules apply to troops in this tribe.

Shoot (x): most troops do not have any ability to damage the enemy at a distance. If a unit is equipped with bows, slings, javelins or other missile weapons then they will have the *Shoot* ability. The number in brackets is the attack value of the unit's shooting attacks.

AMAZONS

Above. Queen Hippolyte and her Guard. The bodyguards are carefully selected for both skill and loyalty.

The female warriors of the Amazon tribes are rightly famed for their skill with the bow as well as their bravery in combat. Their queen, Hippolyte, is recognised by the Gods themselves as one of the foremost warriors in all Greece. Their culture is unique as they are a tribe of women who shun the company of men. They reproduce by taking what they need from male captives, but any male children are abandoned at birth. Only the females are nurtured, and they are trained in all the arts of war so that the tribe can ably defend itself against any who oppose them.

Unit Name	Cost	Type	Models	Movement Rate	Attack	Defence	Special Rules
Hippolyte's Guard	6	Formed	12	6	4	4	Unflinching
Amazons	3	Loose	12	8	5	5	Shoot (6)
Archers	3	Loose	10	8	6	5	Shoot (5)

HIPPOLYTE'S GUARD

The personal bodyguards of the queen are carefully selected for both skill in battle and unwavering loyalty. They fight in the manner of the City-state Greeks, in close battle order, though they are equipped slightly differently. This close order makes them a striking contrast to the swarms of archers who form the rest of the Amazon battle host.

You may only have one unit of Hippolyte's Guard in an Amazon army.

AMAZONS

Some Amazons prefer to get up close and resolve battles in melee rather than by shooting. However, even these warriors carry bows and can shoot at the enemy as they close for combat. This gives them a great deal of tactical flexibility and allows them to adapt successfully to whatever their foes may throw at them.

ARCHERS

Amazon Archers are famous shots, and are common in the army. They are generally the younger or less well-built Amazons, though they can still fight in melee should the need arise. In battle though, their most common tactic is to attack a single target with several units of Archers, breaking each foe in turn before they can close to melee range.

Special Rules

The following special rules apply to troops in this tribe.

Unflinching: units with this ability do not retreat from enemy shooting and will fight to the last man (or Amazon, or Centaur…) regardless of casualties, but their stubborn unwillingness to give ground as a unit is not always the best plan for the individual. If their opponent rolls enough to break them in melee then the unit remains in play. However, a unit that should have broken loses an additional model instead to represent the ones who are killed grimly holding their ground rather than sensibly falling back. *Unflinching* units are not removed when they get to half strength as others are. Instead they continue to move and fight as normal until they are wiped out completely.

Shoot (x): most troops do not have any ability to damage the enemy at a distance. If a unit is equipped with bows, slings, javelins or other missile weapons then they will have the *Shoot* ability. The number in brackets is the attack value of the unit's shooting attacks.

CENTAURS

The hybrid creatures known as Centaurs are often depicted as drunken boors who like nothing better than to turn up uninvited to a feast and cause all manner of trouble. That is entirely accurate. Despite this, or perhaps because of it, they are powerful warriors as well. As a tribe they are somewhat disorganised, but they are always willing to rally to the defence of their homes and are experienced in battle.

Centaurs are gregarious when sober, and many have formed friendships with folk from the City-states, Satyrs and even Amazon tribes. This has taught them even more of the ways of tactics and battle and allows them to fight on equal terms with any other tribe, even when they are more than a little the worse for wear.

Unit Name	Cost	Type	Models	Movement Rate	Attack	Defence	Special Rules
Destriers	3	Loose	8	10	4	4	Drunk
Centaurs	2	Loose	8	12	5	5	Drunk
Colts	2	Loose	6	14	6	5	Drunk, Shoot (5)

DESTRIERS

The oldest and largest of the Centaurs fight in bands known as Destriers. They are considerably tougher and more dangerous than the bulk of the tribe and are no more controllable. They can tip the balance of a battle in a single attack, if they are lucky, destroying a block of Hoplites in a single move. If they are less lucky they can easily be wiped out, as they overreach themselves and end up in a trap.

CENTAURS

The average Centaur is a powerful and dangerous foe, even more so when he has had a few skins of wine. They roam the battlefield in groups, moving swiftly into position to strike. Their strength and weakness is the same thing: drink. It emboldens them and strengthens them, but it also makes planning a Centaur attack a somewhat hit and miss affair. Commonly one unit or other charges off into the fray before the rest of the army is ready. Skilful commanders learn to adapt as the battle flows, making best use of these unpredicted assaults.

COLTS

The youngsters of the Centaur tribes are a boisterous lot who are usually spoiling for a fight. As they have to prove their way in the world before they can inherit, they are eager to get on and do so. However, they are inexperienced in battle and so they are equipped with bows, to participate from the relative safety of a bowshot away. Despite this sensible tradition, few of these energetic youths can contain themselves for a whole battle. Eventually the excitement (and the wine) gets the better of them, and most end up charging off into a melee.

Below. Centaur Destriers can tip the balance of a battle in a single attack, if they are lucky, they can destroy a block of Hoplites in a single move.

Special Rules

The following special rules apply to troops in this tribe.

Drunk: many of the devotees of Dionysus drink to add to their bravery just as they drink to celebrate victories and console defeats. As the battle progresses, these units become increasingly well oiled, adding to their natural belligerence and lack of caution. To represent this, follow these rules. You will need to track the number of the turn you are on for this.

Drunk units always get a bonus number of dice in attack, equal to the current turn number. This is in addition to the larger number of dice rolled by uncontrolled *Drunk* units, explained below.

Drunk units always add the turn number to the number of models remaining in the unit when their opponent rolls a *Test of Courage* for them. Note that this does not affect the point at which they will break for losing half their models.

When a *Drunk* unit is activated, roll a die. If you score a number over the current turn number then everything is fine. You retain control of the unit and may do with it

as you please. However, if you roll equal to or less than the turn number then you temporarily lose control. The unit decides that it is going to have a go at the enemy, regardless of the plan. Roll another die and add that to the normal movement rate of the unit. If the nearest enemy unit is within that distance then they will immediately move to contact and fight it. If not, they will move as close as possible to them.

Uncontrolled *Drunk* units attack in melee with one-and-a-half dice per model in the unit (rounding fractions up). They do not roll any defence dice.

If they cannot make contact, but have the *Shoot* ability, then they will move and shoot with half the dice they normally use. This loss of control is temporary. Roll again at the start of the unit's next activation to see what happens then.

Shoot (x): most troops do not have any ability to damage the enemy at a distance. If a unit is equipped with bows, slings, javelins or other missile weapons then they will have the *Shoot* ability. The number in brackets is the attack value of the unit's shooting attacks.

Above. Young Satyrs are even more badly behaved than human teenagers. This natural waywardness serves them well.

SATYRS

The Satyrs are perhaps best known as drunken and lecherous forest dwellers that prey on lone travellers and luckless maidens. However, you do not survive very long with a reputation like that without learning to fight and

defend yourself. Satyr armies are rare, but do appear on occasions such as when their tribal base is threatened and one of them is sober enough to organise a proper defence.

Unit Name	Cost	Type	Models	Movement Rate	Attack	Defence	Special Rules
Old Soaks	4	Loose	8	6	3	5	Unflinching, Drunk
Dionysians	2	Loose	12	8	4	6	Drunk
Miscreants	2	Loose	10	10	5	6	Drunk, Shoot (6)

OLD SOAKS

All creatures grow old, and Satyrs are no exception. The oldest and wisest of Satyrs are the Old Soaks who have survived quite a few real fights, not just drunken beatings. When they are relatively sober they can be quite formidable fighters, and as their drinking continues during the battle their fearlessness grows to encompass everything. They are few in number, but if you can encourage them towards the enemy successfully they can cause a great deal of damage to them.

DIONYSIANS

With Dionysus as their patron deity, life is one long party for most Satyrs. As mentioned above, this leads them into all manner of fights and every one of them is a veteran of a thousand drunken brawls. For this reason they are fairly inured to the rough and tumble of combat and fight bravely (and often very enthusiastically) even if they are not always sure who or why they are fighting.

MISCREANTS

Young Satyrs are even more badly behaved than human teenagers. This natural waywardness serves them well in battle, where they start by hurling empty cups and amphorae at the enemy and eventually get so drunk that they charge in and start a proper fight. Controlling them is difficult, but no more so than the rest of the army. Use them as a skirmish screen and shoot when you get the opportunity, and try not to be too worried if they charge into an enemy formation instead of providing covering fire. It is just the way they are and you are better served by accepting it and treating the shooting they do manage as a bonus rather than their primary duty.

Special Rules

The following special rules apply to troops in this tribe.

Unflinching: units with this ability do not retreat from enemy shooting and will fight to the last man (or Amazon, or Centaur…) regardless of casualties, but their stubborn unwillingness to give ground as a unit is not always the best plan for the individual. If their opponent rolls enough to break them in melee then the unit remains in play. However, a unit that should have broken loses an additional model instead to represent the ones who are killed grimly holding their ground rather than sensibly falling back. *Unflinching* units are not removed when they get to half strength as others are. Instead they continue to move and fight as normal until they are wiped out completely.

Drunk: many of the devotees of Dionysus drink to add to their bravery just as they drink to celebrate victories and console defeats. As the battle progresses, these units become increasingly well oiled, adding to their natural belligerence and lack of caution. To represent this, follow these rules. You will need to track the number of the turn you are on for this.

Drunk units always get a bonus number of dice in attack, equal to the current turn number. This is in addition to the larger number of dice rolled by uncontrolled *Drunk* units, explained below.

Drunk units always add the turn number to the number of models remaining in the unit when their opponent rolls a *Test of Courage* for them. Note that this does not affect the point at which they will break for losing half their models.

When a *Drunk* unit is activated, roll a die. If you score a number over the current turn number then everything is fine. You retain control of the unit and may do with it as you please. However, if you roll equal to or less than the turn number then you temporarily lose control. The unit decides that it is going to have a go at the enemy, regardless of the plan. Roll another die and add that to the normal movement rate of the unit. If the nearest enemy unit is within that distance then they will immediately move to contact and fight it. If not, they will move as close as possible to them.

Uncontrolled *Drunk* units attack in melee with one-and-a-half dice per model in the unit (rounding fractions up). They do not roll any defence dice.

If they cannot make contact, but have the *Shoot* ability, then they will move and shoot with half the dice they normally use. This loss of control is temporary. Roll again at the start of the unit's next activation to see what happens then.

Shoot (x): most troops do not have any ability to damage the enemy at a distance. If a unit is equipped with bows, slings, javelins or other missile weapons then they will have the *Shoot* ability. The number in brackets is the attack value of the unit's shooting attacks.

Left. This Satyr Miscreant does his skirmishing with a deadly sling.

SETTING UP A GAME

Games are set up in a series of steps:

1) Place scenery.

2) Choose sides of the table to deploy on.

3) Place objectives.

4) Deploy armies.

5) Deal each player three *Hand of the Gods* cards.

PLACE SCENERY

One player places all the scenery on the table. It always looks more interesting if you try to theme the table, or tell a story. Many of the battles at this time were raids on one tribe by another, so perhaps the villages and farms on the tabletop could all belong to one faction. Temples might also be sacred to one of the player's tribes and not the other. Remember not to get carried away and use too much scenery, as you will need enough space between the scenic items to move models about.

CHOOSE SIDES

The player that did not set up the table chooses which side he would like to deploy his army on.

PLACE OBJECTIVES

Starting with the player who chose sides, each player takes turns placing one objective at a time until he has placed both on the board. Each objective must be touching the owning player's table edge, and must be at least half the table width away from the other one (so on a six foot wide table the objectives must be three feet or more apart).

Below. A Greek temple is the perfect item for setting the scene as it is instantly recognisable.

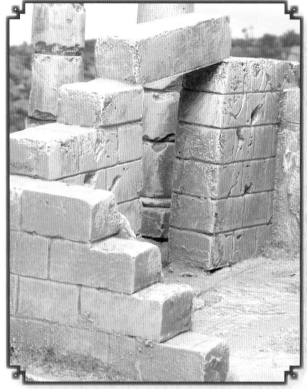

Above. The temple's walls are solid and well built, providing excellent protection from enemy missiles.

DEPLOY ARMIES

In a similar manner to deploying objectives, players take turns putting units on the board, within eight inches of their own table edge. The player to place first is the one with the most units in his army.

SCENERY

In later centuries, hoplite armies preferred to fight across a featureless plain to allow them to best use their tight formations. However, it looks pretty dull in a game, so for *Tribes of Legend* you will need some scenery models to make it look more interesting.

Scenery can be bought or made at home and can be generic or specific. Here you will need a mixture of generic features such as hills and a couple of evocative elements such as ruined Greek temples. Rules for specific types of scenery are as follows:

TEMPLE

A Greek temple is the perfect item for setting the scene as it is instantly recognisable. It forms a barrier to the movement of formed units, but not to loose ones. A loose unit can occupy a temple and even shoot out of it. A formed unit can attack a loose unit that is occupying a temple and if it wins it may drive them out. However, a formed unit can never enter a temple.

A temple's walls are solid and well built and provide excellent protection from enemy missiles. This allows a loose unit within a temple to ignore the first shooting hit against it each turn.

FARM BUILDINGS

The Greek landscape is a rural one, especially in this ancient setting. Farmhouses, shepherd huts and the like are scattered here and there. In game terms they work the same way as temples.

ROCKY OUTCROP OR HILL

These are impassable to formed units, who must move around them. In the game they work the same way as temples, except that the movement of loose units is reduced. When a loose unit wishes to move onto a rocky outcrop or hill it must roll three dice and add the scores together. If the total is equal to or less than its movement rate then it may move onto the scenery at its normal movement rate. If the total is over the movement rate then the unit stops at the edge of the piece of scenery and may move no further this turn. Next turn it may roll again to see if it has found a clear way up.

A loose unit on a rocky outcrop or hill may hide among the rocks and boulders to seek shelter from enemy missiles. This allows them to ignore the first shooting hit against the unit each turn.

STREAM

A small stream poses no obstacle to loose units, but will slow formed ones. A formed unit must end its movement as soon as it reaches a stream. In its next turn it can cross over without penalty and continue its movement.

WOODS

Depending on your scenery collection, you can define the area covered by a wood with a piece of cloth or the base that the model trees are mounted on. In either case, the model trees represent an area of woodland rather than specific individual trees.

A loose unit in a wood may hide among the trees to shelter from enemy missiles. This allows them to ignore the first shooting hit against the unit each turn.

Above. Rocky outcrops are impassable to formed units, who must move around them. Movement of loose units is reduced.

Below. A small stream poses no obstacle to loose units, but will slow formed ones, who must end their movement as soon as they reach a stream.

The game is divided into a series of turns. During each turn, each player will have a chance to move and fight with all of their units.

Each turn is divided into a number of basic steps:

1) The player with the least units left on the table has the initiative first in a turn. In the case of a tie, the player who last moved a unit loses the initiative. Roll a die to break ties on the first turn of the game.

2) The player with the initiative picks one of his units to move, shoot and fight with. This is the "active" unit.

3) Once the active unit has completed its move the initiative passes to the other player, who then chooses one of his own units to act with. This unit now becomes the active unit.

4) Players continue to alternate acting with their units until all of the units on both sides have been activated.

ACTIVATING A UNIT

Each unit in an army can activate once per turn, in any order chosen by the controlling player. Ranges for shooting, movement and so on are calculated when the unit is activated. A unit may be activated and do nothing. However, this still counts as its activation for the turn.

PASSING YOUR TURN

When you have the initiative, you can choose to pass (and do nothing) if at that point you have less units left to activate than your opponent. You continue to take it in turns having the initiative and may later choose to move more units or pass again (if allowed). Passing does not signify the end of your participation for the whole game turn.

Below. The average Centaur is a powerful and dangerous foe, even more so when he has had a few skins of wine. They roam the battlefield in groups, moving swiftly into position to strike.

DECISIONS, DECISIONS...

When you activate a unit it can usually choose between several options. The only time it cannot is if it is already in contact with an enemy unit at the time of activation. In this situation, all the unit can do is make a melee attack against the enemy in contact. If a formed unit is only in contact with a single enemy unit to its flank or rear when it activates, then it will rotate ninety or one hundred and eighty degrees (as appropriate) to face its enemy. This is a free movement before resolving the attack. In all other circumstances the active unit can choose between the following options:

1) Move.

2) Move into contact with an enemy unit and fight it.

3) Move and shoot once.

4) Stand still and shoot twice.

HAND OF THE GODS

The Gods would not be the Gods if they were not meddling in the affairs of mortals. For this reason, each player is dealt three cards at random from the *Hand of the Gods* deck at the start of the game. Each turn a player may play up to one of these cards from his hand. This card may be played at any point while the player has the initiative. The card is used up and will not be replaced, so choose wisely when to call on the aid of the immortals!

Hand of the Gods cards do one of three things:

1) **Haste.** You may immediately act with another unit, without waiting for your opponent to activate one of his (thus acting twice in a row).

2) **Torpor.** You may pick an enemy unit that has not yet activated this turn. That unit is marked as activated and may do nothing else this turn.

3) **Vigour.** Play as soon as you get the initiative at any point in the turn. Pick one of your units that has already acted this turn. It becomes the active unit again and may act as if it had not already done so.

MOVING

Each type of unit has a movement rate shown in the tribal listings. This is the maximum number of inches it may move in its turn. Effects of terrain on movement are explained in the scenery section. If you want to fight someone then you move into base-to-base contact with them during your turn (see below). A model that starts its move in base-to-base contact with an enemy model cannot move this turn.

All movement is measured from the moving unit's leader to the point where the unit wants to go (which can be in any direction you choose). The leader model is then placed at that point and the unit is formed up around him in the normal formation, facing the direction the leader moved. Draw an imaginary line between the starting and end points to define this direction. This means that formed units do not have to bother with wheeling to change their direction of advance. Also, if a formed unit does something fancy, such as changing direction a hundred and eighty degrees and moving to what was its rear, it hardly moves at all as most of the movement is taken up by shifting the leader through the space the unit already occupies.

In addition to the above, a formed unit can also move directly backwards at half rate, retaining its facing.

INTERPENETRATING OTHER UNITS

A moving unit of either type can pass through a friendly unit if the one being moved through is loose. No unit can move through enemy units.

MOVING TO CONTACT WITH THE ENEMY

If a unit wants to move into contact with an enemy unit, then measure the distance between the active unit's leader and either the target unit's leader (if the target is loose) or the nearest model in the target unit (if the target is formed). If this distance is within the active unit's movement rate then it moves to contact. Place the active unit's leader in contact with the target unit's leader (if the target is loose) or with the centre of the nearest unengaged side of the target unit (if the target is formed). Form up the remainder of the active unit around the leader as normal.

A formed unit can only move to contact an enemy unit that was in its front arc at the start of its activation.

A unit will move to contact the side of its target that matches the arc in which the moving leader began his activation. For example, if the leader of the moving unit was in the right flank arc of the target unit when he was activated, then the attack will go in against the right flank side of the target.

Terrain that does not completely block the movement of the active unit is ignored when moving to contact.

There must be sufficient room next to the target to place the active unit once it has moved or the movement is cancelled.

If you move to contact with an enemy unit then you must fight it.

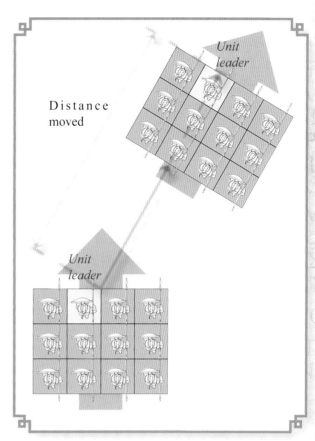

Above. Movement of a formed unit advancing. All movement is measured from the moving unit's leader to the point where the unit wants to go.

Below. The movement of a formed unit turning 180° and moving to its rear.

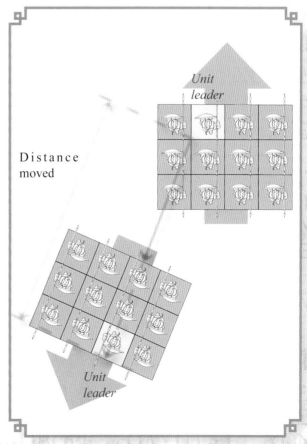

SHOOTING

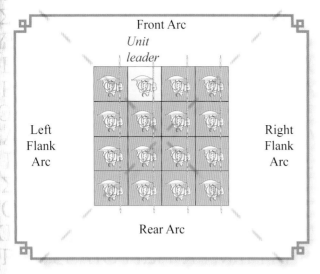

Above. Formed unit arcs of sight.

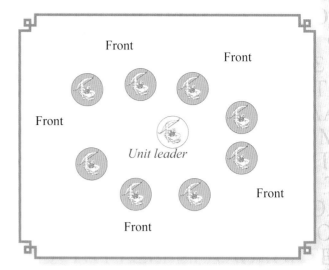

Above. Loose unit arcs of sight.

Shooting is calculated as if the leader of the shooting unit is shooting solely at the leader of the target unit (if the target is loose) or the closest model in that unit (if the target is formed). Calculate all shooting as if it is done only between these two models. However, all attacking and defending models will participate. The sequence for shooting is:

1) Check that you can see the enemy, that you have a clear "line of sight".

2) Measure the distance between the models.

   a. If it is more than a foot then you are out of range and the shots automatically miss.

   b. If the range is less than a foot then continue to step 3.

3) Roll one die per shooting model.

4) Each score that is equal to or over the number in brackets after the shooter's *Shoot* ability hits the target.

5) The target then rolls a die for each model in the unit, trying to roll equal to or over its defence value.

6) Subtract the number of successful defences from the number of successful hits to find the number of models lost. Remove any losses.

7) If a loose target unit takes any losses then it automatically retreats a half-move directly away from the shooter. Formed units do not retreat from shooting.

CAN YOU SEE?

A formed unit can see an enemy unit if the target model is within a ninety degree arc to its front. A loose unit can see all around. In addition, the line of sight between shooter and target cannot be blocked by scenery or models. Hold a tape measure between the shooting leader and his target model (enemy leader or nearest enemy model).

Woods, hills and buildings on this line all stop a shooter from seeing their target. Formed units of either side, and loose enemy units, also block shooting at targets beyond them unless the distant target is raised on a hill or rocky outcrop.

You cannot shoot at a target that is in contact with a unit belonging to your own army.

ARE YOU IN RANGE?

Shooting distance is measured from the leader of the shooting unit to the leader of the target unit (if the target is loose) or the nearest model (if the target is formed). If this distance is less than twelve inches then the shot can be taken.

UNSHIELDED

If the leader model of the shooting unit is mostly in a flank or rear arc of the target unit then the target is being attacked from an unshielded side. Halve the number of defence dice rolled by the defender.

EXAMPLE OF SHOOTING

A unit of six Centaur Colts shoots at a unit of twelve Dionysians. They are both loose units, so the shooter can see all around. The distance between the two unit leaders is less than a foot and there is no scenery between them, so the shot can be taken. The shooter rolls one die per model in the unit and needs '5's and '6's to hit, as the Colts have *Shoot (5)*. The Colts are lucky and score three hits. The Dionysians have twelve models in the unit, so they roll that many dice, needing '6's to match their defence. They roll two '6's. Subtracting the successful defences from the successful attacks means 3-2 = 1 model hit by the shooting. One model is removed from the target unit, which must now be moved a half move directly away from the shooters, as with all loose units that suffer losses through shooting.

MELEE

A unit will fight if its leader is in base-to-base contact with an enemy model after it has moved. See the movement section for rules about moving units into contact. Resolve the melee immediately as part of the active unit's turn. The sequence is:

1) The active unit rolls its attack dice.

2) The target unit rolls its defence dice.

3) Subtract the number of successful defences from the number of successful attacks to find the number of models lost. Remove any losses.

4) If the target unit loses any models it takes a *Test of Courage*.

5) If the target unit survives then the roles are reversed and it becomes the new attacker (even though it is not the active unit) and rolls its attack dice.

6) The new target unit rolls its defence dice.

7) Subtract the number of successful defences from the number of successful attacks to find the number of models lost. Remove any losses.

8) If the target unit loses any models it takes a *Test of Courage*.

9) If the active unit caused losses to a formed target then it remains in base-to-base contact. In any other case the attacker retires a half move directly backwards, out of contact.

ATTACK

A unit fights with a number of attack dice equal to the number of models left in the unit at the moment it makes its attack. Halve this number (rounding fractions up) if the attacking unit is formed.

All dice are rolled at once. Each score that equals or beats the attack value shown on the tribal lists scores one hit.

Below. Centaurs spoiling for a fight with skeletons. Centaurs are gregarious when sober, and have formed friendships with the City-states and even Amazon tribes.

DEFENCE

A unit defends itself with a number of dice equal to half the number of models remaining in the unit (rounding fractions up).

All dice are rolled at once. Each score that equals or beats the defence value shown on the tribal lists cancels one hit from the attacker.

UNSHIELDED

If the leader model of the attacking unit is mostly in a flank or rear arc of the defending unit then the target is being attacked from an unshielded side. Halve the number of defence dice rolled by the defender. In addition, the defender will not get to attack back.

TEST OF COURAGE

If an attacker inflicts losses on its target in melee (not shooting) then he may roll a *Test of Courage*. This is rolled by the attacking player (as it is effectively another form of attack, this time against the will of the defenders) rather than the defender.

Roll two dice and add the scores together. If the target was formed, then add the number of models you just killed to this total. If this total is more than the number of models remaining in the target unit then they are broken and the whole unit will flee. Remove the unit from the game.

ROUTING UNITS

A unit that loses half or more of its initial number of models, for any reason, breaks and flees from the battlefield immediately. Remove the unit from the tabletop. In reality its members are streaming away to the rear, but there is no need to worry about that in the game. The only units that avoid this fate are those with the *Unflinching* ability.

REMOVING CASUALTIES

Models lost from loose units can be taken from anywhere in the unit. Models lost from formed units are always removed from the rearmost rank.

The unit leader is always the last to die.

WINNING THE GAME

Battles are fought until one army flees the field. Each army can sustain a certain amount of losses, but there comes a point at which the warriors have seen too many of their friends fall and turn on their heels to seek safety elsewhere, regardless of the protestations of their general.

As soon as an army has had a total of eight or more *Army Points* of troops destroyed, then the army breaks and they lose the game. Each unit that is lost by falling to half or less of its starting number of models adds its *Army Points*

cost towards this total. Any unit that breaks from combat and is destroyed also adds its *Army Points* cost towards this total. Each objective captured by the enemy counts as two *Points* towards this total. An objective is captured when an enemy unit leader starts a turn in contact with it, and remains stationary in that position for a single activation.

Note that even *Unflinching* units cannot stop this general flight. The army has lost even if a unit or two stages a heroic last stand.

Below. Zeus was the supreme ruler of the Gods. He was primarily a weather-god, using thunderbolts as a weapon. The Gods would not be the Gods if they were not meddling in the affairs of mortals!

HAND OF THE GODS CARDS

The *Hand of the Gods* deck is made up of nine cards, three each of three different types.

### HASTE You may immediately act with another unit, without waiting for your opponent to activate one of his (thus acting twice in a row).	### TORPOR You may pick an enemy unit that has not yet activated this turn. That unit is marked as activated and may do nothing else this turn.	### VIGOUR Play as soon as you get the initiative at any point in the turn. Pick one of your units that has already acted this turn. It becomes the active unit again and may act as if it had not already done so.
### HASTE You may immediately act with another unit, without waiting for your opponent to activate one of his (thus acting twice in a row).	### TORPOR You may pick an enemy unit that has not yet activated this turn. That unit is marked as activated and may do nothing else this turn.	### VIGOUR Play as soon as you get the initiative at any point in the turn. Pick one of your units that has already acted this turn. It becomes the active unit again and may act as if it had not already done so.
### HASTE You may immediately act with another unit, without waiting for your opponent to activate one of his (thus acting twice in a row).	### TORPOR You may pick an enemy unit that has not yet activated this turn. That unit is marked as activated and may do nothing else this turn.	### VIGOUR Play as soon as you get the initiative at any point in the turn. Pick one of your units that has already acted this turn. It becomes the active unit again and may act as if it had not already done so.
### HASTE You may immediately act with another unit, without waiting for your opponent to activate one of his (thus acting twice in a row).	### TORPOR You may pick an enemy unit that has not yet activated this turn. That unit is marked as activated and may do nothing else this turn.	### VIGOUR Play as soon as you get the initiative at any point in the turn. Pick one of your units that has already acted this turn. It becomes the active unit again and may act as if it had not already done so.

You can download the cards from our website: **www.wargamesfoundry.com** *or photocopy them for your own use.*

HISTORY OF THE GODS
WHO'S WHO ON MOUNT OLYMPUS?
MARTIN BUCK

The Greek myths are some of the greatest stories ever told, and some of the most enduring. Originating way back in the mists of time, their characters and storylines are still familiar today, having lost none of their power to shock, move and inspire us.

The Ancient Greeks told these stories for many reasons; to explain natural phenomena that they could not otherwise understand, to flesh out their religious beliefs and the Gods they worshipped to make them more real, to fill in gaps in their history that the passage of time had erased, to glorify their nation or tribe and ascribe a divine lineage to their leaders. Perhaps they also just enjoyed a good story, as we do.

When told together, these myths weave a rich and intricate tapestry where characters and events from one story impact upon those of another. However, from repeated retellings over countless centuries (many of these stories were around long before being written down) divergent, sometimes contradictory, versions have arisen. Because of this, and the huge cast of players involved, the myths can seem impenetrable. So here is a brief introduction to some of the key players. It is by no means exhaustive, but it gives a general idea of who did what to whom, and why, using the most popular versions of these timeless tales.

ZEUS

Zeus was the supreme ruler of the Gods. He was primarily a weather-god, responsible for rain, snow, hail and thunder, using thunderbolts as a weapon. Zeus was the last child of the Titans Cronos and Rhea. Fearing that his offspring would usurp him, Cronos had already devoured Zeus' siblings; Poseidon, Hades, Hera, Hestia and Demeter. Rhea contrived to hide Zeus from his father and the child was able to grow up in safety, eventually overthrowing Cronos and freeing his brothers and sisters. The Universe was then divided between the brothers Zeus, Poseidon and Hades, with Zeus claiming possession of the sky. Although Zeus took his sister Hera as his consort, he had a multitude of affairs with Goddesses, Nymphs and mortals, resulting in numerous children including the mighty Heracles. He ruled the other Gods with a firm hand, often having differences of opinion and punishing them when they transgressed. He also acted as the punisher of mortal wrongdoers. Zeus often took the role of impartial judge in disputes between other deities. The prime example of this is the Trojan War, where he remained objective while his fellow Gods took sides.

POSEIDON

Poseidon was the brother of Zeus and the principal god of the seas and waters. When the sea was given as his domain, he supplanted several older, and kinder, deities and instilled the sea with fear and violence. He is often shown as bad-tempered and dangerous, representing the unpredictability and power of the sea-storm. Odysseus and Minos were just two mortals to feel the wrath of this vengeful God. The first was cast adrift for blinding Poseidon's son, the Cyclops Polyphemus, while the second was punished for neglecting to sacrifice a bull in Poseidon's honour. He filled Minos' wife with passion for the bull. The Minotaur was the horrific result. Poseidon lived in a palace beneath the sea and raced across the surface of the waters in his chariot. He was also known as the god of horses.

HADES

Hades was the god of the dead, ruler of the Underworld. He was one of the sons of Cronos and Rhea and brother to Zeus, Poseidon, Hera, Hestia and Demeter. When the Universe was originally shared out between Hades and his brothers, he was allotted the Underworld for eternity. Consequently he played very little part in the affairs of the living. Hades and his abode were thought of as cold and grim, but he was never considered to be evil or unjust. His greatest involvement in the ancient stories is his abduction of Persephone, daughter of Zeus and Demeter, to be his consort. Although this was carried out with Zeus' consent, Demeter insisted that Persephone should only stay in the Underworld for half of the year.

ARES

Ares was the god of war and the only son of Zeus and Hera. As befitted his title, Ares was frequently depicted as boorish and violent. Only war and slaughter could bring him pleasure so he charged about the battlefield encouraging warriors to greater feats of heroism. Mighty though he was, he could easily be outwitted by Athena who represented thoughtful strategy and genuine battlefield courage. Ares had no wife but indulged in many amorous adventures, often with Aphrodite behind the back of her husband Hephaestus. Eventually Hephaestus caught them out by constructing a net that pinned them to the bed, revealing their affair to the rest of the Gods. Ares supported the Trojans during the Trojan War.

HEPHAESTUS

Hephaestus was the son of Hera. Most accounts say that he had no father. When he was born, Hera threw him out of Olympus because he was ugly and lame. He was found and brought up by Sea Nymphs and during this time he learnt the art of metalworking. Hephaestus gained his revenge on his mother by building her a golden throne that trapped her, and only he had the key to release it. Once they were reconciled he spoke up for her regarding her persecution of Heracles. In a fit of rage Zeus threw him out of Olympus a second time. When he was allowed back he created great works for the Gods, building splendid halls and palaces and creating armour and weapons for mortal heroes such as Achilles. Despite this he was always a figure of fun, partly because of his shambling gait and grubby, sooty appearance and partly because of the way he was continually fooled by his wife, Aphrodite.

APOLLO

Apollo was the god of prophecy, the arts (especially music) and archery. He was also the bringer and dispeller of plagues and therefore became the patron of medicine. He and his twin sister Artemis were sired by Zeus on the Titaness Leto. Apollo's connection with prophecy is best known through his oracle at Delphi. His priestess was named Pythia in remembrance of his slaying of the giant serpentine seer Python. Delphi was thought to be at the very centre of the earth and became the most important oracle of the Greek world. Apollo was a firm supporter of King Priam during the Trojan War and acted as Troy's staunchest defender among the Gods. He gave the gift of prophecy to two of Priam's children and was reputed to have guided the arrow that killed Achilles. Apollo was also known as the bringer of sudden, but natural, death to men.

HERMES

Hermes was a son of Zeus and acted as his messenger. He also guided shades to the House of Hades, protected travellers, brought luck to mortals and was the patron deity of thieves and merchants. He was depicted as a young man wearing winged sandals and carrying a herald's staff. Hermes was frequently attributed with getting his

fellow Gods out of trouble and he accompanied Zeus all over the earth. Like so many of the Gods he conducted numerous love affairs, most notably with Aphrodite and with a Nymph who consequently bore him the god Pan. In his association with the Underworld, it was Hermes who conducted the dead shades of mortals down to the River Styx. He had to take Eurydice back there after her husband Orpheus failed to free her from death and also interceded with Hades to allow Zeus' daughter Persephone back into the world of the living for half of every year.

DIONYSUS

Dionysus was the god of wine and ecstasy. He was accompanied on his travels by Satyrs and Maenads, women who dressed in fawn skins and abandoned themselves to frenzied orgiastic dances. Dionysus was a latecomer to the pantheon of Greek Gods, prompting the belief that he may have been a foreign interloper. Because of this he was originally rejected and persecuted and many cities refused to worship him. In such cases Dionysus' revenge could be terrible, sometimes driving the inhabitants insane so that they fell upon each other and tore each other apart. He was said to have travelled widely outside of Greece; to Phrygia, Egypt and India. It was Dionysus that gave Midas of Phrygia the golden touch after the king had entertained him so well, a gift that turned out to be a curse. From unpopular beginnings, Dionysus eventually eclipsed all the other Gods in popularity.

HESTIA

Hestia was the goddess of hearth and home. She was the eldest daughter of the Titans Cronos and Rhea and refused marriage, despite entreaties from Poseidon and Apollo. She remained a virgin and insisted that her priestesses also adhered to this state. She took no part in the misadventures of the other Gods.

APHRODITE

Aphrodite was the goddess of love, beauty and sexual attraction. She was most commonly thought of as a daughter of Zeus and was the wife of the lame smith Hephaestus. Aphrodite represented passion, and as such she was frequently unfaithful to her husband with other Gods and mortals. She had several children by Ares, including Eros, until Hephaestus managed to trap the two together and presented them to the other Gods for mockery. Aphrodite is largely blamed for setting in motion the events leading to the Trojan War. After bribing the Trojan prince Paris to choose her in a contest of beauty, she made Helen of Sparta fall in love with him and accompany him to Troy. She was a firm supporter of the Trojans throughout the war. While she could help mortals through her gifts of love and attraction she could also punish those who caused her offence, particularly those who claimed to be superior to her in beauty.

Hermes

Athena

Titans Cronos and Rhea. She is best known as the mother of Persephone, whom she bore to her brother Zeus. When Persephone was still a girl, Zeus agreed to give her as a bride to his brother Hades, lord of the Underworld, without consulting Demeter. She was so distraught at her daughter's disappearance that she left Olympus and travelled the world searching for her. While travelling in human form she granted the secrets of agriculture to those who showed her hospitality and developed secret rites for her devoted followers to perform; the Eleusinian Mysteries. Upon discovering Persephone's fate she convinced Zeus to allow her daughter to leave Hades for half the year, when the earth is green and fruitful, and spend the other half in the Underworld, when the earth is barren and cold.

ATHENA

Athena was the daughter of Zeus, patron deity of war but also of many crafts and skills. Her symbol was the owl, a sign for wisdom. Unlike Ares she personified strategy and intelligence as opposed to wild bloodlust. She was invariably shown helmeted with a round shield and spear and a goatskin breastplate; the aegis. According to legend she sprang fully armed and ready for battle from the head of Zeus after Hephaestus split it open with an axe. Athena assisted many brave and wily heroes in their adventures; Odysseus, Bellerophon, Jason, Heracles and especially Perseus. She gave him winged sandals, a wallet and a cap of invisibility to help him overcome Medusa, who had offended her. Athena was a staunch supporter of the Greeks during the Trojan War, even fighting her fellow Gods to support their cause. Her greatest sanctuary was the Parthenon in Athens, a city she only won following a struggle with Poseidon.

ARTEMIS

Artemis was the goddess of hunting and archery, but also the protector of wild animals, children and the weak. She was the twin sister of Apollo and as a daughter of Zeus she gained Hera's enmity. Artemis roamed the countryside with an entourage of Nymphs, vigorously defending her virginity and brooking no interference with herself or her followers. Any mortals who offended her or failed to observe her rites were seriously punished, such as Actaeon who accidentally saw her bathing. In order that he should not tell anyone he had seen the Goddess naked, Artemis transformed him into a stag and he was torn to pieces by his own hounds. Artemis was also known as the bringer of sudden, but natural, death to women.

EROS

Eros was the god of love and desire. He was the son of Aphrodite and her lover Ares. With parents like that it is no wonder he was usually portrayed as a strong, handsome and athletic youth. As time went on he was perceived as increasingly younger, first a mischievous boy and then a winged baby, or even several winged babies. He carried a bow and quiver, giving rise to the belief that some of his arrows were tipped with gold to promote desire and some were tipped with lead to take it away.

HERA

Hera was the queen of Heaven and the wife of Zeus. She was also his elder sister. As one of the children of the Titan Cronos, she was swallowed by her father who rightly feared his offspring would overthrow him. She was set free when Zeus killed Cronos and became Zeus' consort. She was insanely jealous whenever Zeus had affairs with Nymphs and mortals (and he had many) often seeking revenge on the children born from these trysts. The most extreme example of this was her persecution of Zeus' son Heracles, whom she sought to destroy through the instigation of impossible tasks. Hera was a firm supporter of the Greeks during the Trojan War, often helping them against the wishes of her husband. This was largely because the Trojan prince Paris had preferred Aphrodite to her in a contest of beauty. Despite her tendency towards vindictiveness, Hera was worshipped by women all over the Greek world for her strength and chastity.

DEMETER

Demeter was the Earth-goddess, associated with growth and fertility. She was also one of the six children of the

TRIBES OF LEGEND
PAINTING GUIDE
JEZ GRIFFIN

Above. The Gods Hades, Poseidon and Zeus, with Ares and Hephaestus behind them.

Before starting any new project, I take some time to look at all the models and decide on the best approach to painting them. I find it useful to have a few general guidelines in my head regarding style and colour that will help to tie all the models together and make them appear as part of a group. For example, when painting historical irregular types such as ancients, tribesmen, partisans and militia, who are often dressed and equipped in different styles within a unit, I paint one item of clothing on each model the same colour. It could be the trousers on one, the tunic on the next, the cloak on another and so on. This has the effect of making the whole unit appear consistent without using an actual uniform. The same result can be achieved with shield designs and tribal tattoos.

The initial planning stage was particularly important with Foundry's Greek Mythology range as it encompasses a wide variety of weird and wonderful characters, all very different despite their common background in the Greek myths. There are gods and humans in classical Greek attire, monsters that are part human and part beast, and spirits and nymphs taking on human form from natural elements. I really needed a set of simple rules to use as a guide when choosing colours!

I decided wherever possible to give the humanoid characters dark brown or black hair and to use MEDITERRANEAN FLESH 125 as a starting point for the flesh tones to reflect their Mediterranean origin. Their clothing would generally be painted white and off-white. These guidelines formed a good basis from which to start

but, as with all rules, they were sometimes bent or even broken to suit specific situations. I will describe these deviations from the standard colour scheme whenever they occur.

The monsters and spirits were less straightforward. I decided on 'believable fantasy' as my approach to painting this range, so for a model that was half man and half creature, the man part would be painted as per the other human models and the painting for the creature part would be based on its real life equivalent, whether it be bird, goat or reptile! For this to work I needed a technique for blending together the different colours and disguising the join between the human and animal parts. More about that later…

Before painting any of these models I followed the usual basic steps, making sure to clean off all flash and mould lines before anything else. If they are not carefully removed, mould lines will show up through the layers of paint, and any paint thick enough to hide a mould line is too thick! The models were then fixed on individual Foundry MDF bases using superglue for a permanent bond. Once the glue had dried the models were fully undercoated with BLACK paint.

I usually like to get the bases finished before progressing any further with the painting. A small amount of modelling putty was added to hide the join between each model's integral base and the MDF base. Once this had set, PVA glue was applied to the base, being careful not to get any on the feet, hooves or claws of the model or around the edge of the base. This was then dipped into a sand/grit mix while the glue was still wet. Using a variety of larger and smaller grains of sand and grit can produce interesting effects. Once it was fully dry, the sand was painted with BASE SAND SHADE 10A and then highlighted by dry brushing with BASE SAND 10B and BASE SAND LIGHT 10C. I then reapplied the black undercoat where splashes on the model had occurred during basing, being careful not to get any on the newly painted and textured base. Any further basing, such as applying static grass, I left until the models were fully painted and varnished.

KEVIN DALLIMORE'S PAINTING & MODELLING GUIDE

All the models in these guides were painted using Foundry paints with their specially designed layering technique. This technique has been well documented and described in Kevin Dallimore's two Painting and Modelling Guides (both invaluable sources of information, ideas and photographs) and in his article about painting the Cyclopes, so I will not go into too much detail about it here. The standard technique uses three layers applied one on top of the other; shade, mid-tone and highlight. I prefer to use five layers. This is achieved by adding two extra layers mixed from the shade and mid-tone (pots 'A' & 'B') and the mid-tone and highlight (pots 'B' & 'C') which are used in between the standard layers. This gives a gentler transition between the shades; however, the addition of two extra layers does increase the amount of time it takes to paint the models.

I painted the eyes first, neatening up any mistakes by carefully retouching the black undercoat, and then I painted all the flesh tones. For the female models I painted lidded eyes using the flesh tones instead, giving their faces a softer expression. Once all the flesh tones were finished I painted the clothes, starting with those closest to the body and working outwards to the topmost garments. Any belts or sashes I painted last of all.

THE GODS

Being human in appearance, the Gods followed my basic rules of tanned Mediterranean skin, very dark brown or black hair and white clothing. A major point of reference for these was their appearance in films such as 'Clash of the Titans' (the original version).

One detail that needs a special mention is the flaming torch carried by the Goddess Hestia. For this to work I felt the flames needed a more random organic feel than the usual layered method could provide. I started by re-undercoating the flames in white and then picked a selection of paints ranging from very light yellow to very dark red. Starting with the lightest of the yellows and working through to the reds, I applied each colour onto the previous one while the paint was still wet, causing some of the paint to blend and some of it to remain in its original colour. Once I had used the final red in the sequence I let the whole thing dry and then went through the same procedure again. This time I started with white, then the yellows, through to the reds, being more sparing with where I applied the colours. I left the areas where the previous 'wet on wet' sequence

had worked well and over painted the areas that had not, effectively representing the flickering randomness of colours visible in flames.

Clothing	ARCTIC GREY 33
Skin	MEDITERRANEAN FLESH 125
Lips & Nipples	CHESTNUT 53
Hair	EQUIPMENT BLACK 101
Metals (armour, weapons etc)	GOLD 36, GUN METAL 104, ARMOUR 35
Grapes	PHLEGM GREEN 28
Pots & Cups	TERRACOTTA 37
Woodwork	SPEARSHAFT 13
Wheat Sheaf	BUFF LEATHER 7
Sandals	DEEP BROWN LEATHER 45
Torch	WHITE through to RED (as mentioned above)
Apple/Laurels/ Leaves	FRENCH DRAGOON GREEN 70 with PHLEGM GREEN LIGHT 28C for highlight
Snakes	FRENCH CHASSEUR A CHEVAL GREEN 71 with PHLEGM GREEN LIGHT 28C for highlight
Large Fish	TEAL BLUE 24 with SKY BLUE LIGHT 21C for highlight

Below. The Goddess Hestia carrying her flaming torch.

Above. The Gods Apollo, Dionysus, Goddess Aphrodite with an apple, and the Goddess Hestia.

SATYRS

The Satyrs were woodland creatures, renowned for their mischievousness and lustful appetites. Living at one with Nature, they personified its fruitful fertility and were ever hopeful of satisfying their desires with the beautiful Nymphs, whom they pursued relentlessly. The Satyrs accompanied the frenzied women followers of Dionysus, the Maenads, in their drunken revels. Their unrestrained, bestial behaviour resulted in them being given animal attributes; pointed ears, horns, horse and goat legs, and hooves. The Satyrs were closely associated with Pan, the god of pastures and fertility. Pan could be a sinister individual, especially if his sleep was disturbed, but he preferred to play his Pan-pipes while the Nymphs and Satyrs danced.

HARPIES

Although they were originally thought of as ethereal winds, snatching people up and carrying them away, the Harpies were later represented as monstrous bird-like women. The Argonauts encountered the creatures tormenting Phineus, a Thracian king and soothsayer. Every night the Harpies invaded his dining room, stealing food and leaving their foul droppings all over his table. Phineus agreed to prophesy the future for Jason and his crew if they rid him of the monsters. The Argonauts Calais and Zetes, winged sons of the North Wind, chased them off and pursued them until ordered by the Gods to relent, on the understanding they would no longer plague Phineus.

Below. Bird-winged Harpies with wing colours based on birds of prey and carrion birds.

SATYRS

The Satyrs followed my basic rules for part man, part beast characters, with their human parts painted in the regular Mediterranean skin tones and the beast parts based on real animals to make them more convincing. As I started on the flesh, however, I felt the Satyrs deserved an earthier, more unwashed appearance, so I settled upon CHESTNUT 53 for their skin colour instead.

Illustrated colour wildlife guides are an extremely useful resource to have next to your painting table. They are an invaluable source of information with regards to colours and patterns, often providing some surprising possibilities! I based the animal parts of the Satyrs on four genuine breeds of goat: British Togyenburg, British Saanen, Anglo Nubien, and British Alpine. As Satyrs are particularly masculine in nature, I focussed on the male of each breed, paying particular attention to facial patterns, beards and socks (the lower part of the leg, usually black or white in a similar pattern to that of a horse). The one aspect not copied from nature was the horns. In much of my reference material the goat horns appeared very dark. I chose to make them lighter as this worked better with the other colours I had chosen for the models.

Below. Pan and Satyrs with Mediterranean skin tones and the beast parts based on real animals to make them more convincing.

On all but a couple of the Satyrs there was no need to blend the colour transition between the skin tones and the fur. On those that did not have furry legs, and needed some blending, I followed the process described below in the Harpies section.

Flesh	CHESTNUT 53
Legs	STONE 57, DARK AFRICAN FLESH 121, CONKER BROWN 54, DRAB 12, BAY BROWN 42
Horns	RAWHIDE 11
Leather Goods	DEEP BROWN LEATHER 45, BUFF LEATHER 7
Bows	SPEARSHAFT 13
Arrows	SPEARSHAFT 13, ARCTIC GREY 33
Sling Stones	STONE 57
Panpipes	BAY BROWN 42, SPEARSHAFT 13
Pots & Cups	TERRACOTTA 37
Lower Legs	ARCTIC GREY 33, EQUIPMENT BLACK 101
Hooves	RAWHIDE 11 on a white leg, EQUIPMENT BLACK 101 on a black leg

Above. For the bat winged Harpies, the wing structure emerges directly from their bodies.

HARPIES

There are two distinct types of Harpies in the Foundry range; those with bird-like wings and those with bat-like wings. Within these two types there are also a number of variations such as bird legs and claws. As with the Satyrs, I used a slightly different flesh tone for the human parts of the Harpies. This time it was EXPERT FLESH 127, which unlike the majority of Foundry paints has six colours instead of three. It provided a fantastically subtle, slightly pale skin tone that I thought very appropriate for these creatures and it contrasted wonderfully with the colours of the feet and wings.

For the bat winged Harpies, I wanted the wing structure to emerge directly from their bodies, so they needed to start off with a continuation of the skin colour and gradually blend into the grey of the wing. To achieve this I painted EXPERT FLESH SHADE 127A along the main bone structure of the wing as far as the small claw/hand, and halfway along the next bone. The rest of this bone, from halfway along to the tip, was painted with GRANITE SHADE 31A. This produced a distinct line where the two colours met, so the next stage was to paint over the join using a mix of two parts EXPERT FLESH SHADE 127A to one part GRANITE SHADE 31A. Working along from the flesh area into the grey area, this first mix was followed by an equally proportioned 1:1 mix of the two colours and then a third mix of one part EXPERT FLESH SHADE 127A to two parts GRANITE SHADE 31A. As I worked along the wing I made sure that each successive layer left part of the previous layer visible, giving the impression of flesh gradually turning into grey. Painting each layer over a smaller area gives a quicker transition of colour; larger areas give a more gradual one. I then had to add the highlights to this area by repeating the above steps, so each highlight was applied as a three part mix and made to

achieve the same gradual blend as the base colours. I left the black line of the undercoat visible between the bone and the membrane of the wing because I was painting these as two distinctly separate parts.

The same effect could be achieved by using a 'wet into wet' method of painting one colour (the flesh) and then applying the second (the grey) while the first is still wet, allowing the colours to mix at the join. I find, however, that this method can produce a random result of variable quality, best used on areas such as the flames described in the Gods section.

For the bird winged Harpies, I based the wing colours on birds of prey and carrion birds such as hawks, buzzards, crows and vultures. Once again the illustrated wildlife reference material was essential and I used this as an inspiration not just for the colour combinations, but also for the colour patterns amongst the feathers and upon the wings themselves.

Flesh	EXPERT FLESH 127
Feathered Wings	CHESTNUT 53, CHARCOAL BLACK 34, DARK AFRICAN FLESH 121, ARCTIC GREY 33
Bat Wings	GRANITE 31
Hair	EQUIPMENT BLACK 101
Bones, Skulls	RAWHIDE 11
Legs	YELLOW 2, NIPPLE PINK 16, CHARCOAL BLACK 34, STONE 57
Lips, Nipples	NIPPLE PINK 16
Claws	ARCTIC GREY 33

WOOD NYMPHS & WATER NYMPHS

Nymphs were youthful and beautiful female spirits of divine origin who resided in the natural elements. Many were daughters of Zeus and, like their father, they were extremely passionate, having many amorous encounters with Gods and mortals. Although Nymphs were long-lived they were not immortal.

Wood Nymphs lived in and among the trees. Later beliefs spoke of different kinds of Wood Nymphs; Dryads, who could live independently of their trees, and Hamadryads, who resided within a particular tree and eventually died with it.

Water Nymphs were encountered in all bodies of water, from the smallest springs to the wide expanse of the Ocean. The most common Water Nymphs were the Naiads of the rivers and streams. The Nereids lived in the sea. Thetis, the mother of Achilles, was a Nereid.

WOOD NYMPHS

These models are depicted emerging from tree trunks and pieces of wood, something that was always going to be a challenge to paint. I decided to use an alternative method to the one I had used on the Harpies for disguising the blend between the contrasting colours of flesh and bark. I first painted a pine bark texture on the trees. This texture was then carried over onto the human parts of the Nymphs by applying very small rectangles of tree colour to the flesh. These rectangles were applied with varying intensity and were then highlighted. The process was repeated by adding small rectangles of flesh colour among the tree bark. This produced the effect of the two colours crossing over and merging into each other. Both methods of blending contrasting colours can be very effective. I generally decide which to use depending on the texture of the surface I am painting.

Once again I decided to use a paler skin tone as it provided a nice contrast to the woody browns, while the hair was kept dark as per my original colour guidelines.

Flesh	EXPERT FLESH 127
Hair	EQUIPMENT BLACK 101
Wood	BAY BROWN 42, SPEARSHAFT 13B & C
Vine Roots	DARK AFRICAN FLESH 121
Vine & Leaves	FRENCH CHASSEUR A CHEVAL GREEN 71 plus FRENCH DRAGOON GREEN LIGHT 70C
Lips, Nipples, Flowers	NIPPLE PINK 16
Heartwood	BASE SAND 10

Below. Wood Nymphs with paler skin tones giving a nice contrast to the woody browns.

WATER NYMPHS

These models are emerging from water so I used the same technique as for the Wood Nymphs, carrying the colour and texture of the water onto the bodies of the Nymphs, with some flesh tones likewise appearing within the water. In keeping with the previous Nymphs, I used the paler skin colour.

I finished the bases for these models differently to my usual method as it seemed inappropriate to have Water Nymphs emerging from sandy flocked bases! I attached the miniatures to the MDF bases as usual but applied slightly more modelling putty while covering up their integral bases. With a little more water on my sculpting tool than normal, I tried to get a smooth finish to the putty. After allowing it to dry for a little while (but before it had fully set) I used various sculpting tools to gently press a subtle ripple/wave effect onto the surface. Whenever I felt I had gone too far or made any mistakes, I smoothed the surface and started again.

Painting water is never easy and can seem daunting. I started with a very dark PRUSSIAN BLUE 66 and gradually applied highlights. With moving water, such as splashes and ripples, the highlights were easier to place, going along the raised edges as with normal layer painting. The difficulty came with the flatter areas of water, particularly on the bases. Here I decided to apply the highlights in small egg-shaped areas, which gradually overlapped and interchanged with each increasing highlight. These highlights were not necessarily placed one upon the other but rather in a random fashion to give the impression of reflection on the surface of the water. I reapplied small amounts of the darker tones around these same areas and kept repeating the process until I felt it looked right. When painting difficult subjects like water it always pays to have some photographs, drawings or paintings of the subject matter to hand!

Flesh	EXPERT FLESH 127
Water	PRUSSIAN BLUE 66, ARCTIC GREY 33
Foam	ARCTIC GREY 33
Hair	EQUIPMENT BLACK 101
Shells	ARCTIC GREY 33 plus ROYAL PURPLE 19 wash
Lillies	FRENCH CHASSEUR A CHEVAL GREEN 71, FRENCH DRAGOON GREEN 70, NIPPLE PINK 16

Below. Water Nymphs; when painting difficult subjects like water it always pays to have some photographs, drawings or paintings of the subject matter to hand!

Above. Skeletons or Children of the Hydra's Teeth!

CHILDREN OF THE HYDRA'S TEETH

When Jason reached the land of Colchis in his quest for the Golden Fleece, King Aeetes was unwilling to part with it. He set the hero a seemingly impossible task to complete before he would hand over the prize; to yoke a pair of huge bulls to a plough, use them to till a field, sow it with a dragon's teeth and defeat the band of armed warriors that sprouted from them. The warriors started growing from the sown teeth immediately and as soon as they were fully formed they advanced on the hero. Acting on the advice of Medea, daughter of Aeetes, Jason threw a boulder into the midst of the warriors and they began hacking each other to pieces. Jason finished off the last survivors and lived to claim the Golden Fleece.

SKELETONS

The challenge when painting Skeletons, or any other models that are largely one colour, is maintaining the normal attention to detail. If you are not careful the finished models can appear ill-defined. It is easy to become lost in the overall application of a single colour, as opposed to painting other models that have varied items of armour, clothing or equipment, each requiring different colours and individual treatment. I tackled this by painting each Skeleton one section at a time, finishing one arm before moving on to the body, then the next arm, then the pelvis and so on. As I was using the same shades and highlights on each section, there were no concerns about the individual sections not matching once the whole model was finished.

I wanted these Skeletons to appear broken, chipped and fractured, not perfect white sticks! Leaving occasional gaps and breaks while applying the final couple of highlights (I use four or five layers) gave the surface of the bones a rougher texture.

Bones	RAWHIDE 11, BONE YARD 9
Metals	GOLD 36, ARMOUR 35
Linen Cuirass	ARCTIC GREY 33 with BRIGHT RED 15 & SKY BLUE 21 detailing
Wood Fittings	SPEARSHAFT 13

MEDUSA & THE GORGONS

The three Gorgons; Stheno, Eurayle and Medusa, were the sisters of the Graeae. They lived in the far West by the shores of the Ocean. Opinion varies as to the appearance of these creatures. Some traditions say that they were beautiful, even daring to challenge the Goddesses with their looks, but most depictions show them as hideous and terrifying with staring eyes and serpents for hair. Regardless of their looks, one glimpse from a Gorgon, or at least from Medusa, was enough to turn a man to stone. Medusa was pregnant by Poseidon when she was slain and her spilling blood gave birth to the winged horse Pegasus. Perseus gave Medusa's head to Athena, who set it in the middle of her breastplate as a trophy, for she had always despised the Gorgon. The other Gorgon's were said to be immortal.

Right. The three Gorgons; Stheno, Eurayle and Medusa, were the sisters of the Graeae.

GORGONS

The Gorgons were a tricky subject as a major part of them is the transition between the snake and the human, on top of which the texturing of the snake parts had to appear scaly, not smooth and slug-like. I went back to my wildlife reference for images of snakes, particularly head and skin detail. For the serpentine hair, I first painted a line of broken scale-like shapes across the eyebrow region of each snake head. I then did the same around the opening of each mouth and the tops of the nostrils, all the time using roughly rectangular or elliptical shapes. The same shapes were then painted in a line down the centre of each reptile's back and another line down each side of their bodies. Once this was done all the remaining blank spaces between the defined areas could be filled using the same

Below. The Medusa's horrifying visage turns those who behold it to stone!

shapes again. Approaching the subject this way enabled me to define the features and paint a suitable texture without having to meticulously apply a symmetrical pattern to each snake.

I used the same process on the snake half of the Gorgons' bodies except for the tips of their tails, which are quite prominent. I decided to use a contrasting colour and paint them as if they had a rattlesnake rattle, with each segment being highlighted carefully so they would really stand out. The large belly scales were highlighted with strong vertical lines to make them look hard, worn and chipped.

Where the snake and human parts join I used both the colour blending technique from the bat winged Harpies and the technique I had used on the Nymphs of transposing small areas of one colour over the next. This time I used dots of colour instead of rectangles where the green of the snake parts becomes the flesh of the human parts and vice versa.

The statues of the warriors petrified by Medusa's stony gaze were painted a single colour, using the same process as on the Skeletons. Each body part was finished separately before progressing onto the next and any sharper edges were given a very fine highlight to emphasize their hard quality.

Flesh	EXPERT FLESH 127
Snake Bodies & Hair	PHLEGM GREEN 28
Wood Fittings	SPEARSHAFT 13
Metals	ARMOUR 35, GOLD 36
Arrows	EQUIPMENT BLACK 101
Leather Goods	DEEP BROWN LEATHER 45
Rattles	BUFF LEATHER 7
Statues	GRANITE 31

MINOTAUR

When Minos, king of Crete, neglected to sacrifice a handsome bull to Poseidon as he had promised, the God sought revenge. Some writers say that he made Minos' wife, Pasiphae, fall in love with the creature and desire it beyond reason. The Minotaur was the monstrous result of her lust, a creature with a bull's head and a man's body. Minos was so horrified that he had the monster shut away in a specially constructed labyrinth beneath his palace at Cnossos. The Minotaur was eventually killed by Theseus, who gained entry to the labyrinth as part of the nine-yearly tribute of seven boys and seven girls from Athens who were destined to be sacrificed to the creature.

MINOTAURS

Once again my original guidelines came into play, referencing nature for the animal sections and using a Mediterranean skin tone for the human parts. I wanted to paint a variety of different bull heads and so I found reference material for several breeds. I admit they are not native Mediterranean cattle, in fact they are mainly found in the UK, but I thought they would look striking as colour schemes! I did not stick rigidly to the reference material; it gave me a starting point and a good idea of the way the patterns can vary. It was then my job to combine the reference and the models to come up with designs that fitted. The four breeds I used were: Hereford, Highland, Lincoln Red and Galloway.

Despite using MEDITERRANEAN FLESH 125 for the bodies, I decided to use the much paler EXPERT FLESH 127 for any fleshy parts around the muzzles and the faces as I liked the contrast this gave.

Flesh	MEDITERRANEAN FLESH 125
Facial Skin	EXPERT FLESH 127
Fur	ARCTIC GREY 33, CONKER BROWN 54, DRAB 12, CHARCOAL BLACK 34, DARK AFRICAN FLESH 121
Metal Fittings	ARMOUR 35
Wood Fittings	SPEARSHAFT 13

Below. Minotaurs painted with a variety of different bull heads. They are not native Mediterranean cattle, in fact they are based on breeds mainly found in the UK, but they are striking colour schemes!

CENTAURS

Centaurs made their home on the slopes of Mount Pelion in Thessaly. They had the body and legs of a horse, and the torso, arms and head of a man. Although they could be hospitable and friendly they were best known as brutal and lustful, with an irresistible love of wine. The only exception to this common image was the Centaur Chiron who was wise and gentle and became tutor to many of the Greek heroes. The Centaurs famously fought with their neighbours, the Lapiths, after they became drunk at a celebration and tried to carry off the Lapith women. Heracles also had a vicious fight with a group of Centaurs over the contents of a jar of wine, killing many with arrows that had been dipped in the poison of the Hydra.

CENTAURS

Painting Centaurs means painting large quantities of horse flesh! I enjoy painting horses and the Foundry paint range contains a number of ideal colours. There are a few basic rules that I stick to when painting horses; tips and information that I have picked up over the years and found to be a useful guide. I am no horse expert but even if this information is not entirely accurate, it has always served me well.

Hooves and Lower Legs:

I tend to paint the lower legs of most of my horses a very dark brown, almost black. I find this a good solid starting point. Many horse types can have any number of white lower legs (some have none) but I use white quite sparingly. This area can be as small as just the ankle or extend up past the knee and is known by various names depending on the length. I have been told that a black hoof never appears on a white leg and a white/off-white hoof will never appear on a black leg. So my dark brown legs have black hooves and any leg with a white 'sock' has the hoof painted with RAWHIDE 11.

Facial Markings:

Horse facial markings are unnecessary when painting Centaurs but while on the subject of horses it is worth mentioning them. There are a number of different markings a horse can have on its face:

Face: The whole face from the tip of the muzzle (the nose/mouth area) to just beneath the ears and around the eyes is white. The muzzle area can sometimes be pink/flesh coloured. I use EXPERT FLESH 127 for this.

Muzzle: The muzzle area, around the nostrils and mouth is white

Blaze: A broad white stripe down the middle of the forehead from the top of the head to the tip of the nose.

Stripe: A thin white stripe down the middle of the forehead from the top of the head to the tip of the nose.

Snip: A small splash of white, sometimes diamond shaped, from just above the top lip passing between the nostrils and just beyond.

Long Snip: As above but extending to midway up the face.

Star: A small diamond shape of white between the eyes.

Below. Female Centaur Colts. The foreground Centaur has a CONKER BROWN 54 main body colour.

Above. Centaur Destriers.

Horse Types:

Here are my favourite colour schemes for painting horses. Unless otherwise noted, I usually paint the mane and tail a very dark brown/black with mostly black, and occasionally white, socks.

Bays: A bay is a brown horse. The colour can range from a very light tan to dark brown. They have a black mane and tail.

Black: Black horses are usually very dark brown rather than true black. They can, however, have white facial markings and socks.

Skewbald: A skewbald is a white horse with blotches and areas of another colour, usually brown. This can be anything from a mid-brown all the way through to very dark brown/black. Areas of colour can appear randomly but I tend towards a brown head and neck, shoulder areas, and/or thighs and haunches.

Piebald: This is the opposite of a skewbald, a dark brown horse with random white blotches. Their faces are almost always very dark brown/black.

Chestnut: A chestnut coloured horse whose mane and tail can appear the same colour as the body.

White: A white horse sometimes has a white mane and tail, and occasionally a flesh coloured muzzle.

Greys: Anything from a very dark grey to a light off-white, with a mane and tail either black, off-white or grey to match the body.

Palamino: A light brown horse with a blonde mane and tail.

Appaloosa: A dark horse with white back and hind quarters that are in turn covered with dark spots. There is also a leopard coat variety that is either all white with dark spots or all dark with white spots.

The Centaurs carry large Greek shields that I wanted to decorate with a variety of images. I enjoy painting shield designs rather than using transfers. This can seem daunting at first but it does become quicker and easier given a bit of time and practice. The Foundry Compendium contains many images of Greek shield designs and was an excellent reference source when painting these. Having chosen my designs, I painted the face of each shield in a dark shade of the main background colour. Once this was dry I then applied the basic design over the background in a very dark shade of the main design colour. For example, when painting a white horse on a red shield I first painted the shield face a dark red and the basic image of the white horse in a very dark grey. I then built up the image of the horse by adding highlights in exactly the same way as painting a three dimensional model, using each successive highlight to pick out details such as muscles, eyes and ears. If I made a mistake at any stage, I reapplied the previous darker tones to the area and tried again. There is an element of trial and error to painting shields like this but the end result can be some very pleasing miniature images. Once the design was complete I highlighted all the background areas of the shield face that were still visible.

For the human parts of the Centaurs I stuck to the original guidelines I had decided on for human characters; namely tanned Mediterranean flesh and black hair.

Skin	MEDITERRANEAN FLESH 125
Hair	EQUIPMENT BLACK 101
Armour & Metalwork	ARCTIC GREY 33, ARMOUR 35, BRONZE BARREL 103, DEEP BROWN LEATHER 45
Clothes	ARCTIC GREY 33, BRIGHT RED 15, BASE SAND 10
Crests	BRIGHT RED 15, ARCTIC GREY 33, EQUIPMENT BLACK 101
Leather Goods	DEEP BROWN LEATHER 45, BUFF LEATHER 7, TAN 14
Woodwork	SPEARSHAFT 13
Horse Colours	BAY BROWN 42, CONKER BROWN 54, CHESTNUT 53, STONE 57, GRANITE 31, ARCTIC GREY 33, TERRA-COTTA 37, SPEARSHAFT 13

ANCIENT HEROES

GAME OVERVIEW

This is a game of heroic deeds and staggering drunkenness in equal measure. It plays fast and loose with the myths of the Greeks and owes as much to Ray Harryhausen as it does to Homer (no, not that one)! It is a fast, fun and slightly tongue-in-cheek game that can be quickly learned and played using models, scenery and a standard deck of cards. Ancient Heroes is intended for more than two players; it works best with four but can cope with as many as five or six. The more players you have, the sooner the carnage begins!

WHAT YOU NEED TO PLAY

- A collection of mythical Greek models to represent each player's band of heroes. Models should be based individually, but the exact size and shape of bases is unimportant.

- A table to fight the battle on. Six foot by Four foot is about right.

- A Greek temple, ruined or otherwise, to form the objective of the game.

- A selection of other scenery elements to make the landscape more interesting. See below for the different types you can choose from. At the very least you will need one vineyard per player.

- At least one standard deck of playing cards (including both Jokers).

- Two six-sided dice.

- Some small plastic tokens as casualty markers, to keep track of wounds.

SETTING UP THE BATTLEFIELD

The tabletop represents an area of rocky hills in Greece. Exactly how you show this depends on the scenery you have available. The essential element is the temple that forms the objective of the game. This should be placed at the highest point of the battlefield, in the very centre. The terrain should be rockier towards the centre and more arable toward the edges. A spring could be placed anywhere on the table, with a stream running from it to the nearest table edge. The battlefield should include one vineyard per player as these have a particular attraction for the drunks among the heroes. The rest of the scenery is up to you and your collection to determine.

The rocky outcrops should not completely bar the way to the top of the hill, but should offer obstructions and force the heroes to detour around them (unless they can fly).

SETTING UP THE HEROES

All the players' bands of heroes begin the game at an equal distance from the central temple, with the models starting as close to the table edges as they can. The bands

Above. A collection of mythical Greek models represent each player's band of heroes. Models should be based individually, but the exact size and shape of bases is unimportant.

should also be equally spaced around the edges of the board. Exactly how close each group is to its neighbours depends on how many players you have in your game; all that matters is that the bands are as evenly spaced as possible.

SCENERY ELEMENTS

The scenery in this game forms an important part of the challenge for the players, so it is worth getting together a reasonable amount of scenery pieces to keep everyone on their toes. Each element of scenery should be no larger than six inches square (with the exception of the stream). The elements you can choose from are listed below.

In all cases, it is the first model to encounter a particular piece of scenery that has to roll the die to see whether it contains Nymphs, wolves or whatever. After that, models do not need to roll if they approach unless there is a Wood Nymph present, in which case they still have to see if they become transfixed by her beauty or remain focussed on the task at hand. The healing powers of a spring continue throughout the game, if they are present at all.

TEMPLE

Whether this is a working temple or a long-lost ruin is not important. What is important is that it has a clearly defined area so you know whether a model is in the temple area or not. Controlling the temple is the objective of the game.

If the temple is intact then there are no special rules for moving around it. If it is ruined then a model must stop as soon as it reaches the edge of the area. In its next turn, and every turn that it starts within this area, it will move at its normal rate minus the roll of a single die. For example, a human hero would normally move 8 inches a turn. If he rolls a '3' when trying to move through a ruined temple then he will move only 5 inches this turn. If he is still in the area next turn he will roll again to see how far he goes that turn. Each model rolls for each turn separately.

VINEYARD

These are carefully tended and valuable crops and so will be in fairly neat rows and clear of undergrowth. They do not form an obstruction to a hero's movement.

Drunks are attracted to vineyards and the associated wine stores. See the rules for drunken characters below.

Below. A stream could start at the spring and meander its way across the battlefield.

ROCKY OUTCROP

This area of Greece is dominated by rocky hills, so a carefully modelled piece of scenery, rocks from your garden, or whatever else might be easily recognisable as impassable ground is ideal here. The outcrops themselves vary in size, but are typically broken every 6 inches or less and tend not to form long barriers. Instead the paths wind between them, zigzagging back and forth to avoid the overhangs and sudden drops.

Heroes may not move over a rocky outcrop unless they can fly. Even a flying model may not stop on a rocky outcrop, and must have enough movement to move completely past it in a single turn.

BUILDINGS

Tumbledown shepherds' shacks, slightly more comfortable farmhouses and other small buildings are all appropriate, but they should generally be simple and somewhat run-down in appearance. This is a rural backwater rather than a thriving metropolis.

Ruined buildings should use the rules for ruined temples above. Intact buildings are no obstacle to movement, though heroes do have to go around them unless they can fly. Flying over buildings is only permitted if the hero can get entirely across them in a single move.

SPRING & STREAM

A spring could trickle out from behind a boulder or gurgle up from the base of a pool. Either would do nicely here. The stream should start at the spring and meander its way across the battlefield to the nearest table edge, wandering around rocky outcrops and so on as appropriate. It should be no more than an inch wide.

The first time a model moves to within 3 inches of a stream it must stop. Roll a die and look up the result on the table below:

1-2: the stream gurgles quietly on its way.

3-6: a Water Nymph lives in the cool waters. At the end of each turn that a model remains within 3 inches of the spring, it heals a wound.

A stream also has an effect on normal movement. A moving hero must stop as soon as he reaches a stream. In his next turn he can cross without penalty.

SHEPHERD'S CAVE

Unless you have scenery built especially for this game, you are unlikely to have a hill model with a cave in it! If you have collected some appropriate rocks for the outcrops then you could perhaps use some of them to build a cave entrance, or use a circle of black felt or card to represent the cave mouth. This is the only part of the cave that matters here; the murky depths are left for other heroes to explore in other games.

The first time a model moves to within 3 inches of a cave entrance it must stop. Roll a die and look up the result on the table below to see what emerges at the sound of the hero's approach:

1: sheep.

2-3: shepherd.

4-5: wolf.

6: she-wolf.

Place the appropriate model at the cave entrance. What happens next depends on the nature of the hero and the creature encountered.

A human will ignore sheep, fight wolves and lose his next turn regaling shepherds with tales of his bravery.

A Centaur or Satyr will fight wolves and ignore shepherds and sheep.

A Harpy or Minotaur will kill and eat the sheep, attack the shepherd and ignore the wolves (who will flee). You do not need to resolve any combat against the sheep; you can assume the hero will win automatically!

OLIVE GROVE

This represents a small stand of trees rather than a vast forest. All you need is a few tree models; the scragglier the better. It will not generally hinder movement enough to worry about in the game. However, there are sometimes Wood Nymphs lurking inside…

The first time a model moves to within 3 inches of an olive grove it must stop. Roll a die and look up the result on the table below:

1-4: a few birds fly out of the grove, but nothing to challenge a hero.

5-6: a Wood Nymph lives among the trees. Roll a die. On a '1' or a '2' the hero must stay rooted to the spot and try to catch a glimpse of the beautiful creature. Roll each turn to see if the hero can gather his wits and continue. Once

Above. This olive grove represents a small stand of trees rather than a vast forest. However, there are sometimes Wood Nymphs lurking inside…

a hero has passed this test, he is immune for the rest of the game.

Any model that moves to within 3 inches must take this test. If a transfixed model is attacked then the spell is broken and the model fights as normal. Satyrs subtract 2 from their roll each turn as they are particularly fond of Nymphs.

Below. Wood Nymphs live among the trees! Here they are attacked by Cyclopes.

Above. A band of heroes takes possession of the ruined Greek temple, the objective of the game.

CHOOSING YOUR HEROES

Each band of heroes consists of five models and can be Noble, Drunken or Mischievous in nature. Once you have decided which type of band you will be, choose appropriate models as shown in the table below. Not all types of heroes will fight alongside one another and the table lists which types of hero will join each type of group. To make things more interesting, you must choose at least two different types of heroes.

Model	Noble Band	Drunken Band	Mischievous Band
Human	Yes	No	No
Centaur	Yes	Yes	Yes
Satyr	Yes	Yes	Yes
Harpy	No	No	Yes
Minotaur	No	No	Yes

All heroes are armed only with melee weapons, having left their missile weapons at home. Bows and slings are, after all, a far less glorious way to achieve victory.

GAME VALUES OF HEROES AND MONSTERS

Each type of hero or monster (anything that is not a hero) has a set of game values that define their abilities within the game. These are listed on the table below.

HEROES

Model	Movement Rate	Fighting Skill	Armour	Abilities
Human	8	3	2	Noble
Centaur	12	4	1	Drunken
Satyr	8	3	1	Drunken, Favoured
Harpy	8	4	0	Dragon's Teeth, Fly
Minotaur	6	5	0	Monstrous

MONSTERS

Model	Movement Rate	Fighting Skill	Armour	Abilities
Skeleton	6	2	1	Weak
Shepherd	6	1	0	-
Wolf	12	3	1	-
She-wolf	12	4	2	-
Wood Nymph	-	-	-	Beautiful
Water Nymph	-	-	-	Beautiful

ABILITIES

Many models have special abilities to help define them. These are:

Noble: Once per game the hero can call on the Gods to aid him in combat. Your opponent loses either all his attack cards or all his defence cards this round (you choose). Continue the combat as normal.

Drunken: At the end of the whole turn, roll a die for each drunken model still in the game and consult the table below:

1: the hero has a moment of clarity and remains where he is.

2-3: stagger 1 inch.

4-5: stagger 2 inches.

6: stagger 3 inches.

If a model staggers, then it does so directly towards the nearest vineyard.

Favoured: Once per game, during its move, the model can heal all of its wounds. It cannot do this if it has already taken a third wound as it will be dead.

Dragon's Teeth: The model has a handful of magical dragon's teeth that can be sown like seeds to produce unnatural warriors to aid in combat. These can be used once per game at the start of any round of combat. Roll a die and consult the table below:

1-2: false teeth! Nothing happens.

3-5: a Skeleton warrior rises up from where the teeth fell. Place it in base-to-base contact with any enemy model within 3 inches of the model that used the teeth.

6: two Skeleton warriors rise up from where the teeth fell. Place them in base-to-base contact with any enemy model within 3 inches of the model that used the teeth. They may be placed against the same or different models.

Fly: The model can move directly over rocky outcrops, buildings, other models and anything else. However, in order to fly over something it must be able to move completely beyond the obstruction and have space to put its base down on the far side.

Monstrous: The model has five wounds instead of the normal three.

Weak: The model has one wound instead of the normal three.

Beautiful: Nymphs cannot leave the scenery they start in, and cannot be fought. You need appropriate models purely to show which scenery contains them.

Left. Intact temple.

45

SEQUENCE OF PLAY

The game is divided into a series of turns. During each turn, every player has the chance to move and fight with all of their heroes.

Each turn is divided into a number of steps:

1) The player with the model closest to the temple has the initiative. If two or more players have models the same distance from the temple, roll a die to decide who goes first.

2) The player with the initiative moves all of their models, one at a time.

3) The initiative passes to the player to the left of the one who has just moved. This player then moves all of their heroes. Players continue to move their models, one player at a time, in a clockwise order.

4) Once everyone's models have moved, all models in base-to-base contact with an enemy model are dealt their hand of cards and fight until the cards are exhausted, or both players pass.

5) All models that are not in base-to-base contact with an enemy model may move up to 2 inches **if this would enable them to get into contact**. Ignore terrain rules for this movement.

6) Repeat step 4.

7) Check to see if anyone can claim control of the temple. If this is the third consecutive turn a player can claim control then they win the game.

8) Roll for drunken models.

MOVING

Each type of model has a movement value shown in the section on game values. This is the maximum number of inches it may move in its turn. Effects of terrain on movement are explained in the scenery section. If you want to fight someone then you move directly into contact with them during your turn. A model that starts its move in base-to-base contact with an enemy model cannot move this turn.

FIGHTING

A model will fight if it is in base-to-base contact with an enemy model after all movement has been done for that turn. Resolve the fights one at a time, in any order you choose. In games with several players you can sometimes speed things up by fighting simultaneously if there are fights to resolve between different pairs of players.

In a fight, each player is dealt a number of cards equal to the fighting skill value of their model(s). They should keep these hidden from their enemy until they are played.

Players then take turns to play their cards, the player with the most cards going first. If the number of cards is equal then roll a die to decide who attacks first.

The first player chooses to either play an attack card or pass. If an attack card is played then the target player may play a defence card or cards. This defensive reaction is a response rather than that player's turn. His turn will come next, assuming he survives the attack.

Players continue to play cards, attacking and defending until both players have run out of cards or both players choose to pass in succession. This process is done twice in a turn, after each movement step.

Below. Drunken Centaurs attack Mischievous Harpies.

Above. A Noble Band of Humans fights off an attack by Skeletons raised from Dragon's Teeth!

ATTACK

An attack can be made with any red card. An Ace is worth 11 points. All picture cards are worth 10 points. Other number cards are worth their number of points. This number is the strength of the attack. Attack cards can only be played one at a time.

The red Joker is an attack that cannot be stopped.

DEFENCE

A defence can be made with any black card. An Ace is worth 11 points. All picture cards are worth 10 points. Other number cards are worth their number of points. This number is the strength of the defence. Defence cards can be played one at a time or in groups. If played at the same time then their values are added together before calculating whether they have blocked the attack or not.

The black Joker is a defence that will stop any attack except that of a red Joker.

PASS

You can pass your turn at any point during a fight; even if you still have cards you could play. If both players pass one after the other then the round of combat ends. You can still play cards after you have passed in previous rounds if you want to.

RESOLVING COMBAT

When a player plays an attack card their opponent gets a chance to play a defence card(s) to block the attack. Compare the values of the cards:

- If the total value of the defence card(s) is equal to, or higher than, the attack then it has been stopped. It is now the other player's turn to attack.

- If the attack card is higher than the defence value then the attack has hit, but has it caused damage? It now has to get through any armour the defender might be wearing.

Regardless of the result, any cards played are discarded.

ARMOUR

Each type of hero has an armour score, shown in the section on game values. Subtract the total of any defence card(s) played from the attack value. The remainder is the amount that the armour needs to deflect. For each point of armour, draw a card from the main deck (not your hand). Each black card counts towards the defence; red cards are discarded.

If you manage to get a total that equals or beats what is left of the attack, then stop drawing cards as you have successfully blocked that attack. If you draw the full number of cards you are allowed for the armour and have not equalled or beaten the attack, then the target has been hit. One hit equals one wound regardless of whether it was caused by an unblocked ace or just hit by a single point. Use a token such as a glass bead or counter to keep track of this wound.

WOUNDS

All models, apart from Minotaurs and Skeletons, can survive two wounds and die if they take a third. Minotaurs can survive four wounds and will die if they take a fifth. Skeletons are destroyed when they suffer any wound.

COMPLEX FIGHTS

If a fight involves more than one model on a side, then add all the cards for each side together to make a single hand. You still need to declare who is attacking and which foe they are striking, but all the models on one side of such a multiple combat share a single hand of cards.

If more than two sides are in base-to-base contact then work out the fight as several one player versus one player combats.

EXAMPLE OF A FIGHT

A Centaur is fighting a human. The Centaur gets four cards and the human gets three. The Centaur goes first as he has the most cards. He plays a red '7'. In response, the human plays a black '8'. This completely blocks the attack.

It is now the human's turn to attack. He plays a red Queen, which counts as 10 points. The Centaur's only defence card is a '6', and so he plays that. This won't stop the attack on its own so the Centaur needs to draw a card for his armour. Because he played the '6' in defence, this reduces the attack from a 10 to a 4, making it more likely his armour will withstand the blow. He turns over the top card of the deck and gets a black '5' – stopping the attack.

It is now the Centaur's turn to attack again. He plays an Ace for 11 points. The human only has one card left, so unless he has a black Ace or the black Joker he will need to rely on his excellent armour to save him from injury. He only has a red '9', so the Centaur's attack hits home. Humans have an armour score of 2, so he can draw the top two cards to see if it protects him. He gets the other black '8' and a red '6'. Not enough! The human is hit and suffers a wound.

The human fights back with his last card; the red '9'. The Centaur has no defence cards so the attack will hit unless he can draw a black '9' or better for his armour. He gets a red Jack and so suffers a wound.

Finally, the last card either player has is the Centaur's red '2'. The human draws the first of his possible two cards for his armour. It is a black '4' and so the attack is stopped.

Right. Bands of heroes do battle. Noble Bands of Humans and Satyrs prepare to take on a Mischievous Band of Minotaurs right at the foot of the Temple steps. My money is on the Minotaurs!

VICTORY

A player needs to take control of the temple for *three consecutive turns* in order to win. A player controls the temple when they have the only models in it at the end of a turn.

WILD MEN

The world was once filled with strange and dangerous peoples. When the Argonauts stopped off at Bear Island they were attacked by the local inhabitants, the Doliones. Later in their voyage they came to the Land of the Bebryces. Amycus, their savage king, challenged all visitors to a boxing match, and he was so fearsome he always killed his opponent. However, he did not realise that Polydeuces, the champion boxer, was amongst the Argonauts!

Above. Legendary Greek warriors Achilles, Ajax, Odysseus, King Menelaus of Sparta & King Agamemnon.

LEGENDARY GREEK WARRIORS
MARTIN BUCK

AGAMEMNON

Agamemnon, king of Mycenae, was revered as high king by the other Greek rulers. He persuaded Helen's father to give his daughter in marriage to Menelaus, whereupon her other suitors all swore to defend the rights of the man who had won her. Agamemnon reminded them of this oath when Helen was abducted, and led the expedition to Troy to retrieve her. He commanded the Greek host throughout the ten-year siege, but on his return to Mycenae he was murdered by his wife and her lover.

MENELAUS

Menelaus, the younger brother of Agamemnon, was king of Sparta and husband to Helen. He fought a duel with Paris (Helen's abductor) during the final year of the war and would have killed him but for the timely intervention of Aphrodite, who favoured the Trojan prince. Menelaus was furious with Helen and swore to kill her after Troy was taken, but following a long journey back to Sparta his anger subsided and she remained his queen.

ACHILLES

Achilles was the greatest warrior in the Greek army. He was the son of a mortal man and Thetis, a Sea Nymph. When he was a baby his mother dipped him in the River Styx to make him invulnerable, but one spot, the heel where she held him, was left unprotected. During the Trojan War, Achilles argued with Agamemnon and withdrew from the fighting, an act that almost resulted in the defeat of the Greeks. He only returned following the death of his friend Patroclus, slaying Hector, greatest of the Trojan warriors, in a duel. Achilles eventually fell in battle when Paris shot him with an arrow in his unprotected heel.

AJAX

Ajax was a mighty and powerful warrior, second only to Achilles on the battlefield. He was easily distinguished by the huge shield he often carried. As one of Helen's former suitors he followed the Greek war host to Troy where he slew a multitude of Trojans and protected the Greek fleet from a furious counterattack. Following the death of Achilles he was so enraged that he was not given the fallen hero's armour that he plotted to attack his allies. Athena drove him insane so that he attacked and killed a flock of sheep instead, whereupon he was so eaten up by shame that he killed himself.

ODYSSEUS

Odysseus, king of the island of Ithaca, was famed for his cunning. He was unwilling to follow Agamemnon to Troy, even though the oath to defend Helen's husband had been his suggestion to stop the suitors fighting. Once there he proved his worth as a warrior and strategist. Agamemnon sent him to try and persuade Achilles to return to the war, and it was Odysseus who conceived the plan to deceive the Trojans with a wooden horse, which eventually led to the city's destruction. Odysseus was the last of the Greeks to reach home alive. For angering Poseidon he was condemned to drift across the seas, from one peril to another, for ten years. Reaching Ithaca after twenty years away he had to slay a host of suitors who were trying to claim his wife and throne before he could finally rest.

ANCIENT HEROES PAINTING GUIDE

JEZ GRIFFIN

LEGENDARY GREEK WARRIORS

The Legendary Warriors again used my basic rules for human characters, but they also had a lot more equipment to paint. Due to the way some of their armour had been modelled I decided to use other colours than just metals to represent it. For example, on Agamemnon I decided to make the lamellar nature of his armour appear as if made from sections of bone and precious stones. On some of the previous models in the range I had also used non-metallic colours to paint cuirasses, depicting them as linen and leather.

An effective way of showing wealth and status on a model (ancient subjects in particular but not exclusively) is to add patterns to some of the clothing. This can be as simple as a coloured fringe or edging to something as complicated as patchwork patterns and tartans. I used a basic line decoration on the cloak of Odysseus. The main background colour of the cloak (DEEP BLUE SHADE 20A) was painted first. Then, before adding any highlights, I applied the contrasting colour for the line (ARCTIC GREY SHADE 33A) in as careful and accurate a manner as I could. I was neat and tidy on this occasion, but if I had made a mistake, if the line was crooked or uneven, I could have repainted the background colour to tidy it up along the edges or started again. Once the line was mapped out, I highlighted both the background colour and the line colour in the usual way. This was just a single line but the same process applies to stripes and checks. It is easy to make mistakes with details like this but, as ever, practice makes perfect.

I used a lot of bronze on these Heroes. Metalwork can be made to appear richer by adding a further sparkling highlight. In this case I mixed the lightest bronze colour, BRONZE BARREL LIGHT 103C, with another much lighter silvery metal, SPEARPOINT 35C. By applying two or three highlights like this, gradually increasing the amount of silver each time, I ended up with bronze that had a 'silvered' finish. This same technique can be used with many other metals.

Below. Achilles attacks the Bronze Bull.

ACHILLES:

Skin	MEDITERRANEAN FLESH 125
Armour	BRONZE BARREL 103
Metals	ARMOUR 35
Clothes	DEEP BROWN LEATHER 45
Hair	EQUIPMENT BLACK 101
Crest	ARCTIC GREY 33, EQUIPMENT BLACK 101

AGAMEMNON:

Skin	MEDITERRANEAN FLESH 125
Armour	RAWHIDE 11 plus BONE YARD 9 mixed for highlights, ARMOUR 35
Hair & Braids	EQUIPMENT BLACK 101
Clothes	MADDER RED 60
Staff	BRONZE BARREL 103, GOLD 36, DRAB 12

MENELAUS:

Skin	MEDITERRANEAN FLESH 125
Hair	EQUIPMENT BLACK 101
Armour	DARK AFRICAN FLESH 121
Shield	BRONZE BARREL 103
Clothes	EQUIPMENT BLACK 101 plus PHLEGM GREEN 28 in increments as a highlight
Crest	BRIGHT RED 15, ARCTIC GREY 33

ODYSSEUS:

Skin	MEDITERRANEAN FLESH 125
Hair	EQUIPMENT BLACK 101
Armour	BRONZE BARREL 103 plus ARMOUR 35
Clothes	BLACK plus DEEP BLUE 20 in increments as a highlight, ARCTIC GREY 33
Cloak	DEEP BLUE 20, ARCTIC GREY 33

AJAX:

Skin	MEDITERRANEAN FLESH 125
Hair	EQUIPMENT BLACK 101
Clothes	BLACK plus DEEP BROWN LEATHER 45 in increments as a highlight, DRAB 12
Hammer	SPEARSHAFT 13, GRANITE 31, DEEP BROWN LEATHER 45

Above. Underworld Shades.

Occasionally the mythical heroes had to undertake the ultimate voyage, the journey into Hades, the realm of the dead, where they encountered the sad and listless shades of those they once knew. Orpheus braved the misery of Hades in a doomed attempt to bring back his dead wife Eurydice. Odysseus had to enter Hades to consult with the ghost of the seer Tiresias. Fresh blood was needed to entice the ghost to speak, but Odysseus had to prevent a multitude of other shades from drinking it before Tiresias had had his fill. Among these wraiths were his mother and many of his former comrades from the siege of Troy. When Heracles entered the Underworld to take Cerberus he met many shades of the dead including that of the Gorgon Medusa, who terrified the other shades but no longer had the power to cause harm.

UNDERWORLD SHADES

I wanted these characters to appear as shadows, so I decided to paint them entirely in one colour. This would include not just the characters themselves, but all their clothes, weapons, shields and armour. The only exception was their eyes, which I painted plain white without any pupils to gleam in the shadowy sockets. I used the same painting technique on these models as for the Skeletons and the Medusa statues, completing one section at a time before moving to the next.

Entire Model	SLATE GREY SHADE 32A plus BLACK as a base coat, SLATE GREY 32B plus ARCTIC GREY 33 in increments as a highlight
Eyes	RAWHIDE 11 plus WHITE

Below. A group of Satyrs attacks some Underworld Shades.

The wrinkled, grey haired hags known as the Graeae were the sisters of the terrible Gorgons. They had been old from birth and were blind and toothless, except for a single eye and a single tooth which they shared between them. Perseus visited their cave to seek information for his journey to the Gorgons' lair. They were initially unwilling to help, until Perseus forced the information from them by stealing their precious eye.

THE GRAEAE AND PERSEUS

The Graeae, the 'Old Grey Ones'. Grey was clearly an important factor of these characters so I wanted to incorporate it into their appearance. As they are old and haggard a good place to start was their hair. It seemed a little too obvious to carry this over to their clothing, so I decided to use some of the natural earthy colours in the Foundry paint range that would complement the grey of their hair. AFRICAN FLESH 126, DARK AFRICAN FLESH 121 and BAY BROWN 42 were the ideal colours for their rags.

The first two colours I chose raise an interesting point; the versatility of all the paints within the Foundry range. They are designated as African skin tones but they have so many other uses, such as here where I have used them to depict clothing. Other examples that I have used are: CHESTNUT 53 for Near Eastern and Indian skin and for some of the creatures in the Greek Mythology range; PRUSSIAN BLUE 66 used on or mixed with BLACK as a highlight, giving a very rich effect; CONKER BROWN 54 as primarily a horse colour but fantastic on shoes and boots (particularly for Victorians) bags and leather webbing; FRENCH DRAGOON GREEN 70,

my colour of choice when painting foliage such as vine leaves; PHLEGM GREEN 28, fantastic as a skin tone for Orcs and Goblins, or if the shade (pot A) is mixed with a little BLACK, and the mid-tone (pot B) is added in increments as a highlight it is a brilliantly rich alternative to a standard olive grey. Never let the description on the label dictate what you use the paint for. Experiment with different combinations and uses and you will be surprised at the versatility of your paint!

GRAEAE:

Skin	EXPERT FLESH 127
Hair	GRANITE 31
Clothes	AFRICAN FLESH 126, DARK AFRICAN FLESH 121, BAY BROWN 42
Bone	BONE YARD 9
Eye	ARCTIC GREY 33 plus ROYAL PURPLE 19 wash
Cauldron	GUN METAL 104, PHLEGM GREEN 28, BONE YARD 9, MEDITERRANEAN FLESH 125

PERSEUS:

Skin	MEDITERRANEAN FLESH 125
Hair	EQUIPMENT BLACK 101
Metal	BRONZE BARREL 103, ARMOUR 35
Clothes	ARCTIC GREY 33
Cloak	MADDER RED 60

Below. The three Graeae and Perseus. One of the Graeae holds the single eye which they share.

Above. Aeetes - the king of Colchis & his guards.

Reputedly a cruel and ruthless man, Aeetes was the king of Colchis (a region at the south-eastern end of the Black Sea). The Golden Fleece had been given into his care and he was unwilling to hand it over to Jason, particularly as an oracle had prophesied a Greek would kill him. He set the hero a series of seemingly impossible tasks to accomplish before he could have the fleece. With the help of Medea, Aeetes' own daughter, Jason successfully passed the tests. Aeetes, however, broke his promise to hand over the prize forcing Jason to seize it and flee, taking Medea with him. Aeetes pursued but was unable to catch them.

AEETES - THE KING OF COLCHIS & GUARDS

These models depict King Aeetes and his personal bodyguard, so I thought they deserved a uniform appearance. As a king I assumed Aeetes would be fairly wealthy, so this was a good opportunity to include some patterned hems and stripes upon his clothing and that of his men. I used a blue stripe with a white wavy line for the decorative element on the guard tunics. To achieve this I marked the hem out with ARCTIC GREY SHADE 33A and directly onto this applied a sequence of DEEP BLUE SHADE 20A semi-circles, gradually working around the base of the tunic. I wanted them to be a regular shape

and size, so whenever one of them appeared too large or slightly misshapen I neatened it up with the original ARCTIC GREY SHADE 33A, or over painted the mistake and tried again. I found that on the first guard it took me some time to complete the pattern all the way round. I frequently had to correct the blue semi-circles or start them over again, but with some perseverance I made fewer and fewer mistakes. For the last couple of models I hardly had to correct the shapes at all. It was really important to get the pattern right at this stage, with regular spacing between regular shapes. Any mistakes would only appear exaggerated once the pattern was highlighted.

With the basic pattern completed it was a case of highlighting as usual. I highlighted the blue semi-circles first using my normal five stage method, and then the grey parts, all the way through to white. Once the highlights were in place I felt I had a fairly convincing white wavy line on a blue background!

I also wanted a coloured pattern on their hats. I painted each hat with the base colour DRAB 12 first, and then applied the pattern with BLACK, tidying up any mistakes in the thickness of the lines with more of the DRAB 12 base coat. Once happy with the uniformity of the lines and the overall shape, I painted MADDER RED SHADE 60A over the black lines and then highlighted all the hat colours as usual. The same principles work for painting any patterns and shapes on models' clothing and also for painting shield designs. I wanted to keep the rest of their clothes in natural colours as much as possible, using the patterned hems to provide the illusion of wealth.

I used a dry brushing technique on the wicker shields to bring out the fine detail of the sculpted pattern. With dry brushing it is always worth remembering that several very delicate coats are much better than one heavy one. Prior to brushing over the wickerwork area, I wiped my brush on a tissue until there was virtually no colour coming off it. That way the amount of paint applied to the area was almost imperceptible. I repeated this process several times until the highlights began to appear. If dry brushing is rushed by applying thicker paint it can result in clogged detail on the model, blobs of colour and a very messy finish!

Skin	MEDITERRANEAN FLESH 125
Spears	SPEARSHAFT 13, ARMOUR 35
Aeetes' Armour	DARK AFRICAN FLESH 121
Guards' Armour	DARK AFRICAN FLESH SHADE 121A, RAWHIDE 11, BONE YARD 9
Aeetes' Tunic	FRENCH CHASSEUR A CHEVAL GREEN 71B with PHLEGM GREEN SHADE 28A & PHLEGM GREEN 28B as highlights, DEEP BLUE 20
Guards' Tunics	CHESTNUT 53, ARCTIC GREY 33, DEEP BLUE 20
Shields	BRONZE BARREL 103, PHLEGM GREEN 28
Hat	DRAB 12, MADDER RED 60
Sandals	DEEP BROWN LEATHER 45
Aeetes' Cloak	AFRICAN FLESH 126

CYCLOPES

Painting the Cyclopes used all the methods I have previously described, with CHESTNUT 53 providing a wonderfully weather-beaten and unwashed flesh colour!

The one area that needed a bit more attention was the large single eye in each forehead. Being so much larger than normal eyes they needed slightly different treatment to usual. I painted the white of the eye first, this time using ARCTIC GREY SHADE 33A instead of WHITE. I then used a very dark brown to paint in the iris. I made sure that the bottom curve of the iris just touched the top of the lower eyelid, with the upper eyelid coming a little over the top of the iris. If the upper lid comes low over the iris then the eye will appear sleepy or 'lidded'; if the iris is painted as a perfect circle the eye will appear wide and 'manic'. Once I was happy with the placement of the iris I then highlighted the whites of the eye and the iris itself, in this case using lighter browns and then placing a very dark brown or black dot in the centre.

Flesh	CHESTNUT 53
Club Outer Wood	TERRACOTTA 37, SPEARSHAFT 13
Club Heart-wood	BUFF LEATHER 7
Clothing/ Furs	ARCTIC GREY 33, BAY BROWN 42, CONKER BROWN 54, DRAB 12
Eye	ARCTIC GREY 33, DARK AFRICAN FLESH 121

Below. Cyclopes vent their monocular rage.

BRONZE BULL

When Jason reached the land of Colchis in his quest for the Golden Fleece, King Aeetes was unwilling to part with it. He set the hero a seemingly impossible task to complete before he would hand over the prize; to yoke a pair of huge bulls to a plough, use them to till a field, sow it with a dragon's teeth and defeat the band of armed warriors that sprouted from them. The bulls were fearsome fire-breathing beasts that, according to some storytellers, had bronze hooves and bronze mouths, while others told that they were giant, bronze, bull-shaped automata forged by Hephaestus. Jason overcame the bulls thanks to an ointment given to him by Medea, daughter of Aeetes, which protected him from their fiery breath.

Below. The Bronze Bulls were fearsome fire-breathing beasts bull-shaped automata forged by Hephaestus.

BRONZE BULL

This mighty beast was painted almost entirely in one colour, so I followed the same method as for previous one colour models, painting each part separately before moving onto the next.

I used five layers of BRONZE BARREL 103 on the body; the three basic tones straight from the pots, plus two transitional mixed tones in between them to achieve a smooth metallic finish. I picked out all the sharp edges and corners with a much lighter metallic colour to give a crisp sharp effect.

For greater depth I applied a dark brown wash (BROWN WASH 47B) to the deepest recesses. I took extra care with the wash as I only wanted it in specific areas; if it was washed all over the model it would glaze it, changing the tone of all the paints previously applied.

Body	BRONZE BARREL 103, BROWN WASH 47B
Highlights	SHINY 36C
Eyes	MADDER RED 60, BRIGHT RED 15, ORANGE 3

Above. Cerberus guarding the entrance to the underworld. The overall effect on his base was a broken slab floor with the gaps and spaces painted to represent flowing lava.

Cerberus was the watchdog of the Underworld, a monstrous hound from the same brood as the Hydra and Chimaera. He had three heads and, according to some accounts, a serpentine tail and a row of snakes growing along his back. He guarded the gates to the realm of Hades where his main function was to stop the dead from leaving, devouring them if they tried, although he was also charged with preventing the living from entering. Orpheus got past Cerberus by enchanting him with music and Heracles had to use brute force to carry him into the world of the living as one of his Labours.

CERBERUS

The monstrous Cerberus has a paving slab effect on his base. I did consider basing him as normal, giving the integral base a skim of modelling putty to disguise the slabs before adding the usual sand/grit mix for texture. In the end I decided he needed something special, so I used my putty to create further slab shapes on the base, spacing them in a broken fractured pattern with some of the flat MDF base exposed between them. As Cerberus guards the entrance to the underworld the overall effect I wanted was a broken slab floor with the gaps and spaces painted to represent flowing lava.

Once the basing was dry and the model had been undercoated, I painted Cerberus first. He needed to appear very dark with the only real colour coming from his eyes and mouth. The shaggier parts of his fur were dry brushed a very dark brown, being careful to apply several delicate coats rather than a few heavy ones to avoid any blobbing of paint. The same colour was used on the smoother parts of his body but painted here with the usual layering technique to really highlight the bone and muscle structure.

Once Cerberus was complete I painted the lava. Starting with a very dark red, I then applied lighter reds, oranges and yellows, probably around nine or ten layers of paint! I approached the lava painting in much the same way as the water bases on the Water Nymph models, using organic shapes and spots of colour, reworking them until I was happy with the result. The idea was that the lava closest to the slabs would be cooler and therefore a darker colour, with the hotter areas appearing very much lighter. I then painted all the slabs BLACK and highlighted them using a BLACK/DARK AFRICAN FLESH 121 mix. The final effect was a very dark base and creature accented with the bright red eyes, tongues and lava.

Eyes	BRIGHT RED 15, ORANGE 3
Tongues	BRIGHT RED 15, NIPPLE PINK 16
Gums	NIPPLE PINK 16
Body	DARK AFRICAN FLESH 121
Slabs	BLACK plus DARK AFRICAN FLESH 121 as highlight
Lava	MADDER RED 60, BRIGHT RED 15, ORANGE 3, OCHRE 4, YELLOW 2

Above. The whole herd of Pegasi.

When Perseus slew Medusa, the terrible Gorgon was pregnant by Poseidon. Their offspring, the immortal winged horse Pegasus, sprang from the blood that spurted from her severed neck. He roamed the world wild and free, allowing no man to approach or ride him, until Bellerophon sacrificed a bull to Poseidon and was able to tame the steed. With Pegasus' help, Bellerophon defeated the Chimaera.

PEGASUS

When painting Pegasus, or rather the whole herd of Pegasi, I cleaned and tidied the castings first, being especially careful to remove any tiny 'tags' that may have appeared around the fine detailing of the wings. The horse bodies were then based as normal and left to dry. At this stage the wings were still unattached as, due to their size and weight, they needed to be pinned in place. Despite having an integral tag on each wing and corresponding sockets in the sides of the horses (meaning it would be possible to attach them using only these) adding a pin greatly increases the strength of the join and therefore the life span of the model once all the hard work is complete. Failure to pin the wings at this stage could result in a cycle of breaking, re-gluing, repainting, breaking...

Before pinning the parts together I first examined the join, looking at how the integral tag and socket fitted and for suitable points to drill the holes for the pin. As the wing was the most delicate component of the two, I looked along the surface where the join would be made for the thickest point (in this case about 3mm behind the integral tag) as this would offer the most strength for the pin. The pin itself was snipped from a length of heavy duty 1mm wire. Having fitted the appropriate drill bit to my pin vice I carefully started to drill the hole in the wing. When drilling metal models:

- The aim is to make a hole 3-5mm deep.

- Constantly check that the drill is going straight into the surface and not at an angle. Carefully drill a couple of half turns first and then, keeping the pin vice in place, check the angle of drilling.

- Do the above frequently. It is a slow process but better than exiting through a detailed part of the model in an unexpected place!

- Take things slowly. Going at this like a bull at a gate ensures it will all go horribly wrong!

When the hole was deep enough I applied some superglue to the end of the wire pin (not to the opening of the hole) and pushed it into the hole ensuring it went all the way down. At this stage my pin was about an inch long. Once in place I cut it down, leaving 3-5mm exposed.

I then had to drill a hole in the body for the pinned wing to fit into. To make sure this hole was in the correct place I aligned the two pieces and, with the protruding end of the pin in the wing touching the body surface, gently applied a bit of pressure. The pin left a tiny indentation in the surface of the horse body, marking the place to drill! Following the same procedure as before, I drilled into the body, making extra sure that I was drilling straight. Ideally the pin should fit straight, and not bent, for maximum strength. Once the second hole was drilled I checked the fit of the two pieces. I did not apply any glue at this stage; I was just making sure that everything fitted together correctly. They did, the pin in the wing slotted perfectly

wings. The wings are very large but also very detailed, so in order to pick out the fine detail on each feather I decided to dry brush them. Dry brushing is often seen as a quick and easy way to paint a miniature, but when done carefully it is a technique ideally suited to picking out fine detail on a large surface area. It should be approached methodically and slowly. When dry brushing there are a number of points that are worth remembering:

- Use paint that is thicker than normal, something like the consistency of double cream.

- Having dipped the brush into the pigment wipe it on a rag, tissue or similar surface until there appears to be no more pigment coming off the brush. Take care to do this thoroughly as any blobs of pigment hiding within the bristles will apply themselves as blobs of colour to the surface of the model.

- When dry brushing, do so at an angle across the detail of the entire surface to be painted. Then re-dry brush the entire surface from another angle if required.

- The amount of colour applied upon each dry brushing should be minimal, almost imperceptible. If the colour is clearly visible after a single coat then it is being applied too thickly.

- Brush gently, do not scrub.

into the hole in the body. If the pin had been too long, or the hole not deep enough, I could have snipped the pin down to size or made the hole slightly deeper, the second option being the more preferable as the longer the pin, the more secure the fitting.

Once I was happy with the fit I applied superglue to the surface areas of the wing and body and joined the two pieces together. It is sometimes handy at this stage to support the wing/joint with another object, a paint pot, another model, a book, in order to take some of the weight off the joint until the glue is dry. However, these wings had a really good join and a strong pin, so extra support was unnecessary. I left each Pegasus for a couple of hours before repeating the process and attaching the second wing, making sure that the angles of the wings looked fairly symmetrical. Once the second wing was dry I used a tiny amount of putty to cover the joint between wings and body. This further improved the strength of the join, filled any small gaps, and effectively disguised it. I then left everything to dry overnight.

The models were then undercoated and left to dry again. Finally it was time to begin painting and I started with the

Once the wings were finished the main horse bodies were painted in the usual manner. I chose to start with STONE 57B as my shade and then worked my way up sequentially through STONE LIGHT 57C to ARCTIC GREY 33B, mixing pigment from each pot with the next pot in the sequence to create a subtle transition of tones. I did not use ARCTIC GREY 33C (pure white) on the main horse body as I was reserving this for the mane, tail and long hair around the hooves.

Body, Wings, Hair	STONE 57B & STONE LIGHT 57C, ARCTIC GREY 33
Hooves	RAWHIDE 11 plus ARCTIC GREY 33

Below. A herd of Pegasi.

LEGENDARY TROJAN WARRIORS
MARTIN BUCK

PRIAM

Priam was the king of Troy during the Trojan War. He was a gentle old man, respected by Trojans and Greeks alike, pious and capable of great courage. He was kind to Helen when she arrived in Troy while all others showed her animosity. He reputedly had fifty sons and fifty daughters by his principle wife and numerous concubines, of whom Paris and Hector were the eldest. Despite being favoured by the Gods, who protected him when he walked straight into the Greek camp to claim the body of Hector, he perished with his city at the climax of the war.

PARIS

Paris, son of Priam, was a strikingly handsome man, chosen by Hera, Athena and Aphrodite to judge which of them should be awarded a golden apple. He chose Aphrodite after she promised him the most beautiful woman on earth as a prize. While Paris was on a deputation to the palace of Menelaus in Sparta, Aphrodite contrived for Helen to fall in love with the Trojan. They eloped to Troy, setting in motion the tragic events of the Trojan War. Paris did not distinguish himself in the fighting. He was challenged to a duel by Menelaus, which he would have lost but for the intervention of Aphrodite, and later slew Achilles by shooting him in his unprotected heel with help from Apollo. He was later killed by a poisoned arrow, shot by the Greek Philoctetes using the bow of Heracles.

HECTOR

Hector was the favourite son of Priam and generally regarded as the heir to the throne of Troy. He was bitterly opposed to the marriage of Helen and Paris, but served as the Trojan war-leader against the Greek host. When Achilles withdrew from the war following an argument with Agamemnon, Hector led a fierce assault on the Greek ships. Patroclus entered the fray posing as Achilles by wearing his armour to try and rally the Greeks but Hector slew him, taking the hero's armour as a trophy. This act so enraged Achilles that he returned to the war to avenge his friend. He defeated Hector before the walls of Troy and dragged his corpse around the city behind his chariot before dumping it in the dust beside the bier of Patroclus. The distraught Priam eventually persuaded Achilles to give him the body of his son and he took it back to Troy for a proper funeral.

HELEN OF SPARTA

Helen was a daughter of Zeus, who first became the wife of Menelaus, king of Sparta, and then of Paris, prince of Troy. Her beauty was known throughout Greece and there had been many suitors seeking her hand. One of the suitors, Odysseus, suggested they should swear an oath to protect the rights of the chosen husband in order to prevent them from fighting each other. Menelaus was chosen and the oath was upheld years later after Helen succumbed to the trickery of Aphrodite and followed Paris to Troy. Following the terrible Trojan War, Menelaus swore to kill Helen for abandoning him and took her aboard ship to return to Sparta. However, their voyage home was long and troubled and by the time they finally arrived the two were reconciled.

Below. Helen of Sparta and her handmaidens.

Above. Legendary Trojan Warriors battle the deadly Chimaera.

LEGENDARY TROJAN WARRIORS

I approached these models in much the same way as the Legendary Greek Warriors. King Priam's gown provided an excellent opportunity to paint a fabric design on a large flat surface. It took a substantial amount of time to mark out accurately though, as I wanted it to appear as symmetrical as possible. I went back and re-worked the design several times, paying careful attention to spacing and angles, correcting where necessary with either the background colour or the design colour. It was a little frustrating at times but well worth the effort!

Skin	MEDITERRANEAN FLESH 125
Hair	CHARCOAL BLACK 34, ARCTIC GREY 33
Clothes	DEEP BLUE 20, GOLD 36, RAW-HIDE 11, BONE YARD 9
Shields	ARCTIC GREY 33, DEEP BLUE 20, DARK AFRICAN FLESH 121
Armour	TAN 14, DARK AFRICAN FLESH 121, ARCTIC GREY 33, BRONZE BARREL 103, RAWHIDE 11, GOLD 36
Weapons	SPEARSHAFT 13, ARMOUR 35, BRONZE BARREL 103

The Chimaera was one of the many hideous creatures spawned by the monsters Echidna and Typhon. With the forequarters of a lion, the mid section of a she-goat and a snake-like tail, she breathed fire and ravaged the kingdom of Lycia. She was slain by the hero Bellerophon, who swooped upon the monster with the aid of the winged horse Pegasus, and showered her with arrows.

CHIMAERA

This terrifying model truly combined many of the techniques previously discussed! The base was sculpted in the same way as Cerberus', using modelling putty to add some extra paving slabs for a broken floor effect. This time, rather than painting the area surrounding the slabs as lava, the gaps were textured and painted using my usual basing technique.

The wings were pinned in place as I had done with Pegasus. In this instance the goat head was also securely pinned.

When dry brushing the wings I needed to be more careful than normal as I wanted to use three different colours on different parts of the wings, and did not want any splashes of one colour over the adjacent colours!

A couple of places on this model needed a blend from one colour into another, for which I combined the blending techniques used for the bat winged Harpies and the Wood Nymphs.

Wings	DARK AFRICAN FLESH 121, ARCTIC GREY 33, CHARCOAL BLACK 34
Body & Lion Head	DRAB 12 plus WHITE
Goat Head	STONE 57, ARCTIC GREY 33
Horns	RAWHIDE 11 plus BONE YARD 9
Snake Tail	FRENCH CHASSEUR A CHEVAL GREEN 71, FRENCH DRAGOON GREEN 70
Tongue & Gums	NIPPLE PINK 16
Paving Slabs	GRANITE 31

HYDRA OF LERNA

The Hydra, a great poisonous water serpent with multiple heads, was one of the offspring of the terrible monsters Echidna and Typhon. The estimated number of heads ranges from five to a hundred depending on the storyteller, and some say the creature had the body of a hound. The Hydra lived in the swamps of Lerna and was raised by the Goddess Hera for the sole purpose of battling Heracles, whom she despised. Heracles was tasked to slay the monster as one of his Labours, a difficult feat as every time one of its heads was hacked off, two more appeared in its place. He eventually defeated it with the aid of Iolaus (his nephew and charioteer) who quickly cauterised the neck stumps with a flaming brand before more heads could appear.

HYDRA

This model came in several different parts and I found it worthwhile, prior to gluing, pinning, or anything else, familiarising myself with which part went where! There were two types of head as well (beaks open and beaks closed) so I played around with their positioning to see which combination I liked best.

The two neck sections were pinned in place and then the model was attached to an MDF base. The tail was then pinned in place too. I used modelling putty to disguise the joins, being careful to mimic the sculpted surface textures and shapes as closely as possible. The necks already had an integral peg to fit the sockets on the heads so, taking into account the light weight of the heads, I did not feel it necessary to add an extra pin. Modelling putty was again used to cover any visible joins between necks and heads.

I wanted the colours to be as close as possible to those of the Hydra in the famous 1960s film. My memory had this wonderful creation as being green, but watching the film again proved this to be incorrect. The main body appears to be grey/blue with accents of green particularly around the neck/head join areas and reddish purple on points of the body. In one movie poster the Hydra is shown as bright blue… I decided this would not work on the model!

I painted up the Hydra with the usual layering technique, deciding to add the accents of purple and green at the end. I wanted these two contrasting colours to sit comfortably with the grey/blue of the body. If I just applied them straight on to the grey/blue they would have stuck out like war paint or markings rather than appearing as subtle changes in the skin colour. So, for my initial coat I took the purple, or green, depending on the area, and mixed it into a large amount of the main body's grey/blue tone. I applied the green mix around the neck/head join areas and along the spinal ridge of the body. The purple I applied along the raised area between the upper body and the underside scales, carrying this down to the very tip of the tail. Then it was a case of taking the green or purple and adding tiny but increasing amounts to the initial colour mix. Each respective highlight was then added in the usual way, with the final highlights being very close to

pure green and pure purple. Using this method it was possible to add a relatively bright colour to a dark one in such a way that they appeared part of each other. This same technique can be used to depict 5 o'clock shadow, shaven skin or veins in a muscled arm or leg.

As a final touch I took the pure purple highlight and added several drops of clean water to create a very dilute wash. This wash was carefully drawn into and along the joins between each of the intersecting belly plates, which helped further tie all the colours together. Once the wash was dry I decided whether the final effect was striking enough. It was, but if needed I could have added a second wash, and a third, and so on until the desired effect was reached. When using this technique, a more dilute wash is preferable to one that is pigment heavy. A pigment heavy wash is too overpowering and can potentially ruin the model! The wash was only applied directly to the crease in which I wanted it to appear. Had I washed it over the entire surface area of the Hydra's belly and left it to run into the crease, this would have formed a glaze, altering the colours of the whole area. Glazing is an excellent technique and can be used to achieve some very subtle and interesting effects, but it is not what I was trying to achieve here.

Tongues	EXPERT FLESH 127
Eyes	YELLOW 2, CHARCOAL BLACK 34
Beak & Horns	CHARCOAL BLACK 34 plus GRANITE 31
Body	SLATE GREY 32, STONE 57, RAWHIDE LIGHT 11C as a highlight
Body Colour Accents	MOSS 29A plus STONE 57/ RAWHIDE 11 mix, WINE STAIN RED 17 plus STONE 57/ RAWHIDE 11 mix
Belly	RAWHIDE 11

Below. The Hydra. The colours are as close as possible to those of the Hydra in the famous 1960s film!

Above. Minotaurs make fearsome enemies.

Below. A group of Harpies is ambushed by Centaurs with bows and spears.

TRIALS OF A DEMIGOD

This game is modelled on the story of the Twelve Labours of Heracles (or Hercules to our Latin friends). Parts of this story have been included in all manner of fantasy tales and will no doubt be familiar to many of you. Some of the creatures, originally unique to the tale of Heracles, have subsequently spawned whole races of their kin in fantasy games and literature; the Hydra, for example. I have included a brief summary of the main points of each labour to help you through the adventure, but I would urge you to read fuller accounts if you are not familiar with them already as there is no replacement for the original.

The aim of this game is to look at the other heroes who came before Heracles, who tried to capture the Nemean Lion or slay the Hydra and who failed to make it to the ranks of legend. These are the people who built the myth and mystique of the creatures that Heracles so deftly overcame, but for whom no songs are sung.

What if one of these unnamed heroes had beaten Heracles to it? Surely it would be his name that we all knew, and Heracles would be unheard of. So, Hero, let us test that theory. It is time for you to see if you have what it takes to write your name in the pages of history!

GAME OVERVIEW

This is a solo game in which you take the part of a Greek hero in that ancient time when men were men, monsters were monsters, and the Gods appeared as showers of gold or talking waterfalls.

Your challenge is to complete ten tasks set by King Eurystheus (Heracles was originally meant to complete ten tasks, but two more were added by the scheming Eurystheus after he rejected two of the others on technicalities). Each task is supposedly impossible. Heroes, however, do not worry about details like that. The tasks are explained in the following pages and are listed on a set of cards at the end. These cards can be photocopied and cut out so you can shuffle them and draw them in a random order.

The reason for these tasks is complex. Suffice to say that some of the Gods (Hera in particular) have conspired with King Eurystheus to get you killed. To avoid this fate you must complete at least ten tasks, tackling each one as it is drawn from the deck. This is done by matching your Guile and your Strength against the specific problems of that challenge. Some require mostly Strength, while others are more puzzle-like. Most require a mixture of the two.

For some of your tasks you may be assisted by your faithful chariot driver Iolaus. How much you rely on him is your choice but King Eurystheus takes a dim view of people helping you and may discount challenges that you complete with Iolaus' help. The game requires careful management of resources, mainly your Strength and Guile, but also Iolaus and the aid you may request of the Gods. By careful use of these diverse resources, and with a bit of luck, you will be able to complete ten or more tasks and redeem yourself in the eyes of the Gods.

As a final note, for the sake of simplicity the term 'monster' is used for anyone you have to fight, regardless of who or what they are.

WHAT YOU NEED TO PLAY

- A model of a Greek hero to represent yourself, and another model for your chariot driver Iolaus.
- A collection of models to fight against – see the individual tasks for the requirements.
- A small playing area to act out the more complex fights.
- A small amount of terrain to make the battles more interesting. Bits of ruined Greek temples and so on would be ideal.
- Some six-sided dice.
- Pen and paper.
- The set of cards for the twelve challenges (included at the end of this game).
- The set of counters representing the *Hand of the Gods* (included at the end of this game).

PREPARING YOUR CARDS & COUNTERS

Photocopy the cards and counters provided for your own use. They will work as paper, but will survive handling better if you stick them to card. I prefer using a cheap pack of normal playing cards to stick them to so that the backs match and they are all identical sizes. They usually shuffle better than homemade ones too. Rub off any excess glue from the fronts of the cards and try a few practice shuffles to smooth things out and make the deck shuffle better in play.

Once you have prepared your cards, they need to be shuffled and placed in a stack, face down, ready to be drawn.

Counters can be stuck to thin card, such as cereal packet card. They do not need shuffling; the card is just to make them more robust and less likely to blow about during play.

SETTING UP TO PLAY

You do not need a large playing area for your heroic deeds. If you have a little scenery and some models then it will look more exciting. The models are used to show the relative positions of warriors during fights, and who has the advantage in combat. The scenery is decorative rather than functional. Put the hero model in the centre of your playing area with the other models, dice, cards and counters to hand. Note your starting values for Guile and Strength on the notepad, then shuffle the challenge cards and draw the top one when you are ready to begin.

SEQUENCE OF PLAY

The game is divided into a series of challenges, or labours, each of which must be completed before the next one can be undertaken. Between the challenges there is a phase where the hero can recover from his wounds and perhaps rebuild his depleted strength. The sequence is: challenge, rest, challenge, rest, and so on until the challenge deck is exhausted or the hero dies.

Each of the challenge stages is divided into a number of steps:

1) Turn over the top card in the deck of challenges.

2) Decide whether to accept the challenge or to use the *Hand of the Gods* to place it at the bottom of the deck and draw another. Repeat step 1 & 2 until you have accepted a challenge to undertake.

3) Decide whether or not to take Iolaus with you on the challenge.

4) Roll to determine the omens for the challenge.

5) Take up to five turns to complete the three or four Acts of the challenge. Each time you roll on Strength or Guile, you use a turn.

6) If you have successfully completed the challenge then go to step 7, otherwise you have failed.

7) Roll to see what reward you may claim.

In each turn you may roll either Strength or Guile dice, but not both at once (unless allowed to do so by the *Hand of the Gods*).

If at any stage your hero dies or you fail a third challenge, then you have lost the whole game. If Iolaus dies then you may continue on your own. If you have not completed the last Act of the challenge by the end of the fifth turn then you fail it and it is placed to one side. There is no shame in failing these tasks; after all they are considered impossible and many have failed before you. However, you must complete at least ten challenges to fulfil your obligations to Eurystheus (and the Gods) and win the game.

Rest stages are much simpler than challenges. All your wounds are healed in a rest stage. In addition you recover ten dice worth of **either** Guile **or** Strength (not a mix). Decide which you will take and make a note of your new totals accordingly. You cannot exceed your initial total with this recovery, so any excess is lost.

RESOURCES

The game revolves around using your Strength and Guile to overcome the various challenges you face, and calling on the Gods for aid only as a last resort. In addition, you have your faithful chariot driver Iolaus to help you.

Strength and Guile are both represented by a number. This is the total number of dice you can roll for that ability. However, these dice are used up when you roll them and only come back when you rest (see above). This means that you have to carefully calculate how many you need to roll and try to save what you can for later challenges.

In a challenge you will be told to do something like 'roll 6 on Guile' or 'roll 24 on Strength'. This means that you need to roll a total of the stated number (or more) using dice from the appropriate pool. Your Guile and Strength totals are cumulative between turns. For example, when trying to 'roll 6 on Guile', you would have to choose a number of dice to roll from your current total of Guile. You would want to be pretty sure of success so would perhaps choose two dice. This would reduce your Guile total by 2. You would then roll the dice and hope to get a total score of '6' or more. If you failed, you would have to roll more dice in the next turn to add to the total, reducing your Guile again by the number of extra dice you have rolled.

At first it may seem as if rolling all your dice at once is the answer, but this is deceptive. You do not replenish all your dice between challenges and will need to save what you can. At the same time all of the challenges have a limited number of turns to complete them, so you need to balance speed with careful management of your resources.

STRENGTH

You are a mighty hero with the strength of several men. You are also well versed in the arts of war and have fought, and beaten, many strange creatures. To show how strong you are you have a pool of dice representing your remaining Strength. This will go down and back up again during your adventures, but can never be more than fifty. You start with 50 Strength.

GUILE

Although heroes are known mainly for their Strength, it is often their Guile and low cunning that shows them the way to beat the monster or achieve the impossible. What use is Strength if you do not know where or how to apply it? To show how cunning you are you have a pool of dice representing your remaining Guile. This will go down and back up again during your adventures, but can never be more than fifty. You start with 50 Guile.

WOUNDS

When you are attacked by a monster you may be wounded. While you will undoubtedly press bravely on, you are not immortal. You start with no wounds and die if this total gets to fifty or more. Between challenges you recover fully and so will begin each new challenge with no wounds again.

HAND OF THE GODS

Being a Greek hero, it is inevitable that the Gods will take some part in your fate. To represent this, you start the game with three *Hand of the Gods* counters. Each of these can be used only once, but will allow you to do something that is otherwise impossible. When you choose to play one you must select the effect you wish from the following list:

- You may place the challenge card you just drew at the bottom of the deck (instead of discarding it as you would if you had failed) and draw another.

- The Gods allow you to use both Strength and Guile in one turn (instead of just one or the other).

- You may re-roll all of the dice you just rolled. You must keep this new total (unless you spend another *Hand of the Gods* counter to re-roll it all again). This could be a roll of a single die for omens or a reward, or a handful of many dice for Strength or Guile.

- The Gods protect you from harm. For one turn you suffer no wounds.

- The influence of the Gods buys you a little more time. You get an extra turn to complete this challenge.

IOLAUS

Your companion is not a famous warrior like yourself, but he is able to help in a variety of circumstances. This aid is represented by a pool of ten dice that can be used instead of (or as well as) your own Guile and his total will be added to yours. This pool recovers at a rate of three dice per rest stage. Iolaus is weaker than you and will die if he takes a total of only twenty wounds. Like you, he completely recovers any damage he has taken during the rest between challenges.

During a challenge he may roll for Guile in the same turn you roll for Strength. Iolaus has no Strength value and will not damage these legendary foes even if he fights (though he can be killed in battle by monsters).

If Iolaus helps in a task, roll a die when it has been completed. On the roll of a '1' or '2' Eurystheus decrees that you had too much help, and rejects this challenge. It does not count towards the ten you must complete to win the game.

OMENS

Before you embark on any challenge you must pay your respects to the Gods and consult the oracle to find out whether the omens are good or ill. Sometimes the Gods will smile on you and other times they will cause you all manner of disaster. Whatever happens, they must be consulted. Roll one die and do as the omens suggest.

FIGHTING

Fights are resolved by rolling a particular number on Strength, while your monstrous opponents are rolling dice to wound you, as explained in the individual challenges.

When you are fighting a monster you will be trying to gain the upper hand and to angle for a better position. A fighter in such a beneficial position is said to have the advantage. The function of the models is to show who has this upper hand. Do this by placing a model with the advantage behind its opponent. When fighting a number of opponents you may be in a position where the hero has the advantage over one of the monsters while a second has the advantage over him. Keep track of each independently. These situations are much easier to follow with the use of models.

A hero or monster gains the advantage in the following turn if they roll more '6's than their opponent when fighting. This means that nobody has the advantage on the first turn of a fight. The effect of having the advantage is that it allows you to re-roll fighting dice. If you have the advantage then you can re-roll whichever dice you choose. If a monster has the advantage they will re-roll any dice result of a '1' or '2'.

When fighting several opponents at once, you may only deal with one per turn. Your opponents, on the other hand, may all attack you each turn.

If Iolaus is present he will not be attacked by the monsters unless the challenge says he will. On the whole he tries to stay out of your way.

THE TWELVE LABOURS

Each challenge has a number of sections to help you play. These are:

Introduction: how you approach the task.

Background: what the challenge is all about.

Omens: the results of the omens that are consulted at the start of each challenge.

First, Second and Third Act (and in one case a Fourth Act): the stages you need to undertake to complete this challenge. You must complete these in order. You may carry over Guile or Strength totals from turn to turn, but not from Act to Act.

Reward: what, if anything, you can take away as a reward for completing this task.

THE NEMEAN LION

You have killed lions in the past during hunts so this does not sound too hard. Of course the local peasantry claim its skin is impervious to arrows and it cannot be stopped, but they always say things like that when they want one of their betters to do their dirty work for them!

BACKGROUND

A huge lion has been terrorising the area around Nemea for many years and local hunters have failed to capture or kill him. Rumours have spread of the power of this beast, which can supposedly change its shape and is protected by the Gods so that it cannot be hurt. King Eurystheus wants this pest destroyed.

OMENS

Before you start the challenge, roll one die and consult the oracle:

1-2: *The crown rests lightly upon the brow of the dead king.* The omens are confusing and misleading. You need to roll '6' on Guile to unravel what they mean before you can start your first turn.

3-4: *The saviour of the people is at hand!* You are just the hero for the job. Good luck!

5-6: *Greet your foe as a brother.* Ignore weapons and wrestle the beast. You count as completing the first two Acts without using any Guile dice. Start your first turn at Act 3.

FIRST ACT

Initially things go well; tracking the lion seems simple enough. When you find it you try shooting it with your bow. Roll '5' or more on Guile to realise that the lion's pelt cannot be pierced.

Below. If you cannot use weapons then you are not afraid to wrestle the lion with your bare hands. Against this it has no insurmountable defence.

SECOND ACT

If sharp weapons cannot damage the beast, then perhaps blunt ones will. You attack the menace with your cudgel. Now you are close, the lion can fight back. You take seven dice of wounds each turn. Roll '9' on Guile to convince yourself that this is not going to work either and come up with a better plan.

THIRD ACT

You are the strongest man alive. If you cannot use weapons then you are not afraid to wrestle the lion with your bare hands. Against this it has no insurmountable defence. Although it too is strong, you can beat it. Roll '35' on Strength to finish the beast and rid the locals of this blight. However, because you cannot use weapons you must subtract 1 point from each die you roll before adding it to the total. You are badly raked by its claws as you wrestle it, though it cannot fight as well once you have it in your grip. Take five dice of wounds each turn.

REWARD

If you beat the Nemean Lion, roll one die and consult the table below:

1: When you come to look at it closely, the lion's pelt is mangy and unkempt and is worthless as a trophy. You get nothing.

2-5: Using the lion's own claw to remove the skin your weapons cannot cut, you take the pelt and wear it over your shoulders to proclaim your victory. It is so tough that you can reduce each attack dice that is rolled against you by 1. For example, if the Hydra attacks you and rolls '2', '4', '5' you will take only 8 damage, not 11, as each die is reduced by 1 before it is added together.

6: You gain the pelt of the Nemean Lion as above. In addition, your heroism has so impressed the Gods that you gain an additional *Hand of the Gods* counter if you currently have less than three.

THE LERNEAN HYDRA

This does sound like a difficult fight. If two heads replace each one you cut off, you will have to be very quick to hurt this beast. It also has poisonous blood, so even wounding it is dangerous. All told, you had probably better take Iolaus with you, as you will need all the help you can get. Perhaps he will have a good suggestion.

BACKGROUND

The swamp-dwelling serpentine Hydra lays waste to its surroundings and terrifies the locals. Its poisonous venom and seven heads make it a fearsome opponent, but its most dangerous weapon is the peculiar ability to grow two new heads whenever one is destroyed.

OMENS

Before you start the challenge, roll one die and consult the oracle:

1-3: *The land is weeping.* Doom and disaster reign! Everyone is down-hearted. Roll '7' on Guile to persuade Iolaus to come with you. You must use your own dice to do this and only get one chance. Choose the number of dice to roll carefully.

4-5: *The Gods know all!* While things seem terrible, and the Hydra is a fearsome monster, the Gods have a plan.

6: *Abundance withers in the fires of sacrifice.* Something about this sounds helpful. You may re-roll any dice you wish in the first Act.

FIRST ACT

When you chop off one of the Hydra's heads, two more immediately grow back in its place. Until you have rolled '15' on Guile to fathom out a way around this you cannot pit your might against the beast.

SECOND ACT

With skill and speed you discover that the heads do not regrow if the wound is burnt quickly enough to seal it. Ideally this can be done by Iolaus whilst you chop off the heads, but it is just possible to do it on your own. Roll '21' on Strength and '9' on Guile to chop off the first three heads. Meanwhile, you take four dice wounds each turn from the splashes of the Hydra's poisonous blood and another four dice from the bites.

THIRD ACT

You have badly weakened the Hydra, but it is not yet beaten and will fight to the last. Roll '15' on Strength and '6' on Guile to remove the last heads. Meanwhile, take three dice of wounds from the searing blood. If Iolaus is with you the Hydra will attack him instead of you on a roll of '4', '5' or '6' on a single die. Whoever is attacked takes three dice of wounds.

REWARD

If you beat the Lernean Hydra, roll one die and consult the table below:

1-3: The stinking corpse of the Hydra slips back into the swamp before you can examine it. You get nothing.

4-6: You dip your weapons in the poisonous blood of the dead Hydra. You may choose to use these poisoned weapons in any one future fight to the death. This poison allows you to re-roll any Strength dice that roll a '1' or a '2'. You must keep the second result (unless you re-roll it again with a *Hand of the Gods* counter). The poison lasts for the whole fight, but has worn off by the end.

Left. The Hydra lived in the swamps of Lerna and was raised by the Goddess Hera for the sole purpose of battling Heracles, whom she despised.

THE CERYNEIAN HIND

A deer? That is bound to be the easiest task of all. Ah, not if it is that deer. How do you kill something that is the favourite of a Goddess without angering that Goddess?

BACKGROUND

Eurystheus realises that you can probably kill any of the powerful monsters he sends you against, so he devises a more insidious plan for your demise. The Golden Hind of Ceryneia is sacred to Artemis. By killing it (which is not easy in the first place as it can outrun an arrow) you will incur Artemis' wrath and she will kill you in turn.

OMENS

Before you start the challenge, roll one die and consult the oracle:

1-3: *Disaster and dismay await you on this path.* The omens are terrible! Use a Guile die to roll again on this table. Keep using Guile dice until you manage to get a better result than this.

4-5: *The wise man sees the good in all he meets.* All will be well. The Gods have a plan.

6: *You are only mortal.* You are only doing the Gods' will. Killing the hind is not your choice, so you cannot be blamed for it. Once you have captured the hind and completed the second Act you have completed this task; you do not have to roll for the final Guile total in the third Act. Artemis will heal the hind and guide you to Eurystheus who must accept her will.

FIRST ACT

You are told by Eurystheus that you must kill the hind to complete this challenge. To do this you must first devise a plan to snare the creature as it runs faster than an arrow. Roll '25' on Guile.

SECOND ACT

Once you have devised your plan and ensnared the hind, roll '5' on Strength to injure it so that it cannot escape.

THIRD ACT

At this point you will need to roll a new total of '25' on Guile to reason with Artemis and avoid her wrath. If you do all this then you will have completed the task.

REWARD

If you capture the Golden Hind, roll one die and consult the table below:

1-5: You are lucky not to incur the wrath of Artemis. You get no reward but your life.

6: Your genuine contrition and subservience to the Gods impresses Artemis and she forgives your hunting of her pet. You gain an additional *Hand of the Gods* counter if you currently have less than three.

Above. Greek heroes Achilles and Ajax about to begin the quest.

THE ERYMANTHIAN BOAR

Boars are stubborn and violent creatures with sharp tusks and a vicious temper. Killing one is hard, but taking one alive could be much more difficult. You will need a cunning plan…

BACKGROUND

A huge and fearsome wild boar has been causing chaos in the area around snowy Mount Erymanthus where it has its lair. Eurystheus sets you the task of capturing this dangerous beast and bringing it to him alive.

OMENS

Before you start the challenge, roll one die and consult the oracle:

1-2: *The mountains do not care about a grain of sand.* Mount Erymanthus is large and wild and there are thousands of places the creature could be hiding. You need to roll '9' on Guile to find the beast before you can even start the first Act.

3-4: *All creatures are the children of the Gods.* The boar is no more blessed than you are; the Gods know you can capture it.

5-6: *A brave heart overcomes a strong arm.* When it sees your determination, the boar ceases its struggle. You complete the third Act automatically, without the need to roll or to take a turn to do so.

Below. The Gods Athena, Hera, Demeter, Artemis and Eros.

FIRST ACT

Instead of trying to bludgeon the boar senseless, you decide to try to tire it out first. However, it is a sturdy creature and you will need to roll '39' on Strength to tire it out.

SECOND ACT

Having exhausted the boar you force it to go to ground. Roll '12' on Guile to drive it from its lair and into deep snow where it will flounder.

THIRD ACT

The final stage is the easiest, with a mere '5' Guile needed to net the creature, who is stuck in a snowdrift.

REWARD

If you capture the Erymanthian Boar, roll one die and consult the table below:

1-5: You present the boar, still alive, to Eurystheus, who cowers terrified in a half-buried pot. He really does not want the boar, so you let it go. Eurystheus admits you have completed the challenge, but that is your only reward.

6: Having completed the challenge you offer Eurystheus the boar, but he tells you to dispose of it yourself. You make it an offering to the Gods, and they are so pleased that you gain an additional *Hand of the Gods* counter if you currently have less than three.

THE AUGEAN STABLES

Eurystheus must be enjoying this. Having given up on seeking your death for the moment, he now seeks the destruction of your honour. Cleaning up animal muck is peasants' work, not that of heroes, regardless of whether it is in a lowly hovel or the greatest stables in the world. Mind you, there may be a way to turn this to your advantage.

BACKGROUND

Having tired of trying to kill you with monsters, Eurystheus finds an equally impossible task, but one that involves unpleasant and demeaning labour instead of combat. He tells you to travel to the court of King Augeas, who owns more cattle than anyone else in Greece, and to clean out his vast dung-filled stables in a single day.

OMENS

Before you start the challenge, roll one die and consult the oracle:

1-2: *The elements rise up in anger.* The omens are poor. You need to score '6' on Guile in each of the second and third Acts in addition to the roll needed on Strength.

3-5: *A great flood.* It is a time for heroes and noble deeds. You will do well.

6: *Earth and water offer themselves as a sacrifice to you.* You may re-roll your dice for Strength in a single turn of this challenge. You must re-roll all or none of the Strength dice for that turn; you cannot choose to be selective as you normally can.

FIRST ACT

Roll '9' on Guile to convince king Augeas to give you a tenth of his vast herd if you can complete this task in a single day. You arrange for his son to witness your triumph.

SECOND ACT

The cleaning of the stables is actually quite simple for someone of your strength and cunning. Of course, you won't actually be shovelling any of the muck yourself. Roll '19' on Strength to tear down two opposite walls of the enclosure.

THIRD ACT

You then need to roll '16' on Strength to dig trenches that divert a nearby river through the stables. The huge rush of water that ensues flushes out the filth and detritus and drains away. You have cleaned the stables.

REWARD

If you clean the Augean Stables, roll one die and consult the table below:

1: Augeas refuses to honour his agreement, even when his own son tells him you have completed your end of the bargain. In addition, Eurystheus decides to discount this challenge because you agreed to be paid for it like a common labourer. You get nothing.

2-5: Augeas refuses to honour his agreement, even when his own son tells him you have completed your end of the bargain. You get nothing but the satisfaction of completing the task.

6: You gain a tenth of the largest herd in Greece, and immediately offer it to the temple for the Gods. They are impressed by your gift and in return you gain an additional *Hand of the Gods* counter if you currently have less than three.

Below. The Gods Apollo & Dionysus.

THE STYMPHALIAN BIRDS

Eurystheus can see that you are a match for any single monster so he has sent you to fight a flock of birds. How are you supposed to do that? You might as well try to fight the wind!

BACKGROUND

Yet another of the natural menaces that seem to plague the countryside is the flock of Stymphalian Birds. Some say they are killers of men, shooting people down with their steel-tipped feathers and pecking them with steel beaks. Others say that they are so venomous and evil that even their droppings are poisonous. They make their lair near a lake in a remote part of the countryside, and strike out from there to ravage local farms. You must somehow kill them or drive them off.

OMENS

Before you start the challenge, roll one die and consult the oracle:

1-2: *The sky eats the land and all is lost!* The omens are dreadful and you must have them recast. You need to score '9' on Guile to persuade the oracle to offer more libations to the Gods and re-examine the omens. Roll the die again for the omens. If you get this result again then you will have to persuade him to try a third time.

3-4: *Thunder from the land and all is well.* The omens are less than clear, though they seem to be promising and you embark on your challenge without undue worry.

5-6: *Steel is weak.* You need to reconsider your battle gear when fighting unusual foes. You are inspired to talk to the locals who offer you protective clothing made from cork, which they say will resist the sharp beaks better than your usual armour. If you are attacked in Acts 2 or 3 then you only take half the wounds (round up) each turn.

Above. Mosaic of killing the flock of Stymphalian Birds. The Birds must somehow be killed or driven off.

FIRST ACT

You eventually find their hideaway and can see the birds in the distant trees around the lake, but it is inaccessible on foot. The ground near the lake is too swampy and treacherous for you to cross. The task seems impossible. You must use a *Hand of the Gods* counter to petition aid from the divinities. If you cannot or will not use one then continue to the second Act anyway.

SECOND ACT

If you spent a *Hand of the Gods* counter then Athena sees your plight and gives you a rattle made by Hephaestus – craftsman to the Gods and God of the forge. Roll '44' on Guile to make enough noise to scare the Stymphalian Birds into the air. If you have the rattle you may double the total you roll in each turn. A few of the bravest birds fight back rather than flee, giving you three dice of wounds each turn. If Iolaus helps then he takes half the damage (round down).

THIRD ACT

As the birds rise up you draw your bow and shoot them down. There are a great number of them and they will attack if they see a chance. Roll '44' on Strength to kill enough of them to drive away the survivors. You take twelve dice of wounds each turn from their steely beaks that pierce your armour.

REWARD

If you drive off the Stymphalian birds, roll one die and consult the table below:

1-3: A few smelly bird carcasses are of no use. You will have to accept the glory as its own reward.

4-6: The locals are so pleased that they throw a banquet in your honour. You are wined and dined with the best the region has to offer and regain an additional five dice of Strength as you rest between this challenge and the next.

THE CRETAN BULL

Above. Ajax fights the bull.

Capturing a bull does not sound like an especially complicated challenge. It is not magical, does not bleed poison and cannot fly. Perhaps Eurystheus has been lenient for a change?

BACKGROUND

Having offended Poseidon by failing to sacrifice his bull, King Minos of Crete has had his lands ravaged by the creature, which rampages through crops, destroying farms and terrorising the population. Eurystheus sends you to capture the creature and bring it back alive.

OMENS

Before you start the challenge, roll one die and consult the oracle:

1-4: *Calm the waves with your blood.* Poseidon is angered. To cross safely to Crete in order to bring back the bull you must sacrifice one of your *Hand of the Gods* counters. If you do not have one then you automatically fail this challenge.

5-6: *Rise up in joy, the ancient king is returned!* Happy villagers greet you wherever you travel. This does not actually help at all, but it makes you feel more heroic.

FIRST ACT

To get to the bull you must first cross the waters. Roll '5' on Strength to stomach the sea crossing.

SECOND ACT

Following the trail of destruction is not difficult and you easily find the huge Cretan Bull. It is a massively strong and beautiful creature and you are glad you do not have to kill it. It is, however, as dim as it is handsome, and you only need to roll '12' on Guile to sneak up on it.

THIRD ACT

You leap on the bull, catching it unawares. In order to wrestle it to the ground and tether it you need to roll '46' on Strength. For the first turn you automatically have the advantage. You take ten dice of wounds per turn as you are stomped by its hooves and stabbed by its horns.

REWARD

If you capture the Cretan Bull, roll one die and consult the table below:

1-5: When you return, Eurystheus is annoyed that you succeeded yet again. He orders you to release the bull, which you obediently do. Being a creature of habit it simply goes back to causing its familiar destruction; this time around the city of Marathon. You gain nothing.

6: Eurystheus reluctantly acknowledges your success and tells you to get rid of the bull, but neglects to say how you should do this. Before he can change his mind you sacrifice it to Poseidon, as Minos should have done years earlier. You gain an additional *Hand of the Gods* counter if you currently have less than three.

DIOMEDES' HORSES

The four horses of Diomedes are probably the strangest of chariot teams in all Greece. You are not sure whether Eurystheus actually wants them to race with or whether they are simply another dangerous task for you to undertake. Not only do you have to deal with the horses themselves, but Diomedes won't be happy either.

BACKGROUND

Diomedes, king of the Bistonians, has a team of four man-eating mares and Eurystheus wants you to steal them. Whether they eat human flesh because they are wild or whether this bizarre diet has driven them crazy is hard to tell. In either case, you will probably have to fight the guards as well as the horses to complete this challenge.

OMENS

Before you start the challenge, roll one die and consult the oracle:

1-2: *The wise man trusts to nature and the Gods.* This seems to mean that you should have faith in the natural way of things. Perhaps an innocent young groom will calm the temper of the wild horses. Subtract 2 from your reward roll if you complete the challenge.

3-4: *Blood, blood, blood!* This task is dangerous. Take care!

5-6: *Swords can also cut those that wield them.* You are warned of the impending doom and are especially careful when dealing with the horses. Add 2 to your reward roll if you complete the challenge.

FIRST ACT

You must fight Diomede's guards to get close to the horses. Roll '13' on Strength to kill them or drive them off. The guards make poor warriors and can inflict no wounds on you.

SECOND ACT

Having reached the stables, you capture the tethered horses. They are fiery-tempered and hard to handle and you will not be able to get them back to your ship quickly enough to avoid Diomedes. Roll '11' on Guile to keep them safely restrained whilst you fight Diomedes, who is sure to come and try to recapture them.

THIRD ACT

You must fight Diomedes and two of his best men. Roll to fight each separately; one per turn. To beat Diomedes you need to roll '23' on Strength. He inflicts eight dice of wounds per turn on you. To beat his henchmen you need to roll '11' on Strength against each of them. They each inflict three dice of wounds on you per turn. Note that you cannot carry over dice rolls from one fight onto another in this challenge. If you beat them all then you can return to your ship.

REWARD

If you manage to steal the horses from Diomedes, roll one die and consult the table below:

1-2: While you are fighting, the groom you left with the horses is trampled and killed. You raise a city in his honour, which is very noble, but means that you do not get to rest between this challenge and the next.

3-5: It turns out that Eurystheus does not want the horses for himself, and he releases them into the wild when you return. You end up with only the glory for completing the challenge.

6: You are allowed to keep the horses for yourself. This has no game effect, but would make a great chariot conversion for your hero model to ride in!

Below. A herd of Pegasi is attacked by a group of Minotaurs.

THE BELT OF HIPPOLYTE

Fighting women to steal their clothes is more than a little demeaning, and presumably this is why Eurystheus has suggested this task. It would be best if she could be persuaded to part with it without a fight, but women can be fickle…

BACKGROUND

Hippolyte is queen of the Amazons; a tribe of warrior women. The belt was a gift from Ares, the God of war, as recognition of her prowess in battle. If you have to fight her for it there will be an epic struggle. Hopefully you can explain to her that you are on a divine mission and she will part with it peacefully.

OMENS

Before you start the challenge, roll one die and consult the oracle:

1-3: *Beware the woman scorned.* You have not seen Hippolyte yet, so it cannot mean her. You think it refers to the Goddess Hera, who hates you. In every fight of this challenge, your opponent starts with the advantage in the first turn.

4-5: *The cooking pot is hot. Take care when you pick it up.* Nobody seems to have the vaguest idea what this means.

6: *The serpent's hiss is your mother's love.* You know Hera will work against you, so you are prepared. In the second Act you may re-roll dice each turn as if you had the advantage in a fight.

FIRST ACT

As you are handsome as well as strong and cunning, you decide that the best approach is part negotiation, part seduction. However, before you can do that you must make a peaceful approach and be welcomed. Roll '7' on Guile to get close to Hippolyte.

SECOND ACT

Hippolyte is torn between your manly charms and the influence of Hera. Each turn Hera's influence will equal five dice. You must beat this roll with your Guile in order to persuade Hippolyte to give you the belt. Hera's total is cumulative between turns, just like yours.

THIRD ACT

As you have persuaded Hippolyte to go against her wishes, Hera stirs up the other Amazons to fight you. You have no choice but to quickly kill the unsuspecting Hippolyte, take the belt and make a break for it. You must fight three of the bravest Amazons to get back to your ship and escape. Roll to fight each separately; one per turn. To beat each Amazon you need to roll '14' on Strength. They each inflict five dice of wounds on you per turn. You cannot carry over dice rolls from one fight onto another in this challenge. If you beat them all then you can return to your ship and sail away with the belt.

REWARD

If you take Hippolyte's belt back to Eurystheus, roll one die and consult the table below:

1-3: You feel bad about killing Hippolyte treacherously and brood about it as heroes do. Only recover five dice this rest turn as your mind is much disturbed.

4-5: Eurystheus gives you the belt of Hippolyte in order to avoid Hera's wrath. It is much too small for your broad frame, and so you offer it to the temple of Hera yourself. She is furious. Lose a *Hand of the Gods* counter. If you do not have one left to lose, lose 5 points of Guile and Strength instead.

6: Eurystheus gives you the belt of Hippolyte in order to avoid Hera's wrath. It is much too small for your broad frame, and so you offer it to the temple of Hera yourself. She is somewhat placated and you gain an additional *Hand of the Gods* counter if you currently have less than three.

Left. Hippolyte, queen of the Amazons.

THE RED CATTLE OF GERYON

Above. The Goddesses Athena and Hera.

You cannot complain about the opportunities for travel as a hero. This task will literally take you to the end of the earth.

BACKGROUND

Geryon is a monstrous fellow with (depending on whose description you believe) three heads, three pairs of legs and the ability to fight with three sets of weapons at once. He lives at the end of the world and it is his famous red cattle that you are supposed to steal and bring back to Eurystheus.

OMENS

Before you start the challenge, roll one die and consult the oracle:

1 2: *The tiniest detail is the work of the Gods.* This is not about the wonders of creation, but the meddling of Hera. If you manage to defeat Geryon and take the cattle, she will send flies to pester and enrage the cattle so that they wander off and are difficult to control. Once you have finished Act 3, you must still roll '7' on Guile to get back safely and count this challenge as complete.

3-4: *Fine is the voice of the master!* Despite the protestations of the oracles, they clearly have no clue what this means.

5-6: *Open your eyes to win the battle.* Be ready to learn from the foreign barbarians you encounter. Add 2 to your reward roll if you complete this challenge.

FIRST ACT

Travelling to meet Geryon is a challenge in itself and involves crossing a vast desert. Roll '11' on Strength to reach Geryon's distant lands.

SECOND ACT

As soon as you arrive you are greeted by a fearsome two-headed watchdog. Roll '9' on Strength to beat the hound Orthus. If Orthus gets to fight back he will cause three dice of wounds per turn. After one turn of fighting Orthus, the herdsman Eurytion comes to his aid. Roll '7' on Strength to beat Eurytion. He will cause two dice of wounds per turn he fights.

THIRD ACT

Having slain the guards, you are now confronted by Geryon himself. He causes nine dice of wounds per turn and you must roll '33' on Strength to defeat him. If you do so then you may capture his cattle and drive them back to Eurystheus.

REWARD

If you beat Geryon and take his red cattle, roll one die and consult the table below:

1: You are exhausted when you return after years of adventure. You do not benefit from a rest between this challenge and the next.

2-3: You return the cattle to Eurystheus who promptly has them sacrificed to Hera. This seems to help his standing with the Gods, but does nothing for you.

4-6: All your experience with strange and far-flung peoples at the ends of the world has taught you some new tricks. You get an additional 5 points of Guile (up to your maximum of 50).

The Goddess Hera

THE GOLDEN APPLES OF THE HESPERIDES

Above. The Gods Hephaestus, Ares, Zeus, Hades & Poseidon, with The Garden of the Hesperides behind.

Stealing from the Gods themselves sounds like the most difficult of tasks, as there are many fearsome guardians to face. Of course, you have to discover where the Garden of the Hesperides is before you get to that stage.

BACKGROUND

The Garden of the Hesperides is a location concealed at the edge of the world. In it is a tree that bears golden apples; a present from Gaia (the Earth) to Hera when she married Zeus. It is guarded by a hundred-headed dragon, Atlas the Titan, and the Hesperides themselves (the 'Daughters of the Evening', sometimes said to be the daughters of Atlas). Even finding the place will be a challenge.

OMENS

You do not consult the oracles for this challenge. After all, why give the Gods any more warning of what you are planning than you have to?

FIRST ACT

The exact location of the garden is a closely held secret and it takes years to find out who knows about it. Eventually you find the ancient God Nereus and wrestle him to make him divulge its whereabouts. Roll '15' on Strength to hold him long enough to persuade him to tell.

SECOND ACT

Having discovered the garden's location and made the arduous journey, you find that you cannot reach the apples yourself. To get them you must trick Atlas, the Titan who bears the weight of the heavens, into plucking them. Roll '17' on Guile to get him to pass the weight of the sky onto your shoulders and pick the apples for you.

THIRD ACT

Having persuaded Atlas to pick the apples, he now decides that he does not want to carry the sky on his shoulders any more; he will let you do that while he delivers the apples to Eurystheus himself. Roll '33' on Guile to trick Atlas into taking the weight of the heavens again (while you adjust your cloak) so you are not stuck there for eternity.

REWARD

If you steal the golden apples, roll one die and consult the table below:

1-6: Eurystheus is surprised that you have succeeded and nervous that he is now in possession of items stolen from the Gods themselves. He promptly returns them and you are both lucky not to be struck down by a thunderbolt.

CERBERUS ⊠ THE HOUND OF HADES

Of all the challenges, this must be the most terrible. Fighting for your life is one thing, but starting a challenge where you are guaranteed a visit to the Land of the Dead is quite another. You only hope you can fathom how to return.

BACKGROUND

Cerberus is the three-headed hound that guards the entrance to the Underworld. He is not evil as such, but he is a fearsome and deadly foe. Even just getting to him is a huge undertaking as nobody has ever returned from the Land of the Dead before. You are to bring him back alive.

OMENS

Before you start the challenge, roll one die and consult the oracle:

1-6: *The way is dark.* The oracle is afraid that you will die very soon. Beyond that he cannot say.

FIRST ACT

You cannot take Iolaus with you on this challenge. No mortal has ever returned from Hades alive, and taking a companion in there would be far too risky. You cannot be sure whether you can return at all, let alone with him. To begin the challenge, you seek out priests who know the Eleusinian Mysteries to find out how you might return from Hades – the Land of the Dead. Roll '8' on Guile to devise a plan to survive this adventure.

Below. Cerberus, the three-headed hound that guards the entrance to the Underworld, faces a heroic adventurer.

SECOND ACT

You enter the Land of the Dead and travel past uncounted souls in various torments. They try to trick you into staying there. Roll '17' on Guile to see through their tricks and continue.

THIRD ACT

In order to avoid offending any more Gods than you have to, you seek out Hades – Lord of the Underworld. You explain your task and ask his permission to take Cerberus to the surface. Roll '7' on Guile to get him to agree to your taking Cerberus, though he makes the condition that you cannot use any weapons to subdue him.

FOURTH ACT

Finding Cerberus is no trouble as he guards the entrance faithfully. Beating him is another matter. Roll '41' on Strength to capture him. However, because you cannot use weapons you must subtract 1 point from each die you roll before adding it to the total. Take six dice of wounds each turn.

REWARD

If you return with Cerberus, roll one die and consult the table below:

1-2: You are greatly saddened by seeing so many fallen comrades in torment. You do not get a rest turn between this challenge and the next as you seek to cleanse yourself at the temple.

3-6: You have consulted with the dead and returned from Hades to tell the tale! You get an additional 5 points of Guile (up to your maximum of 50).

THE NEMEAN LION

THE LERNEAN HYDRA

THE CERYNEIAN HIND

THE ERYMANTHEAN BOAR

THE AUGEAN STABLES

THE CRETAN BULL

THE STYMPHALIAN BIRDS

DIOMEDES' HORSES

THE BELT OF HIPPOLYTE

THE RED CATTLE OF GERYON

THE GOLDEN APPLES OF THE HESPERIDES

CERBERUS THE HOUND OF HADES

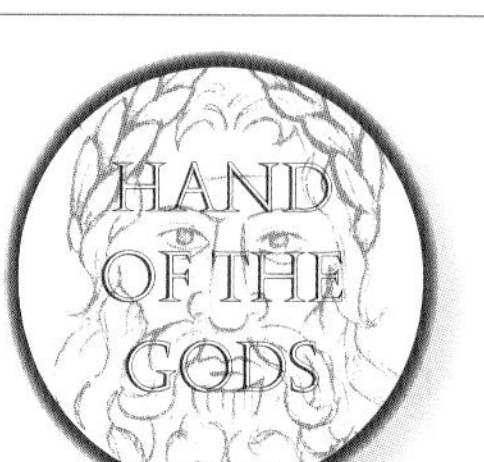

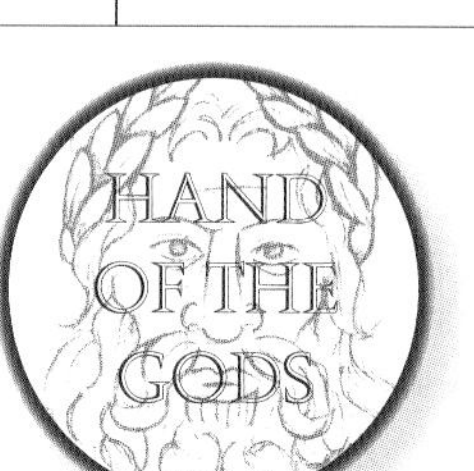

HAND OF THE GODS

HAND OF THE GODS

HAND OF THE GODS

HAND OF THE GODS

HAND OF THE GODS

Download the cards and tokens from our website: **www.wargamesfoundry.com**. *or photocopy them for your own use.*

Above. Ajax and Achilles battle the terrifying Harpies.

Below. Amazon archers may have bitten off more than they can chew by attacking the Hydra.

AMAZONS
PAINTING GUIDE
JEZ GRIFFIN

Above. The Amazon Chariot.

AMAZON CHARIOT

I constructed and painted the Amazon Chariot in several stages. As ever the first job was to check all the parts and carefully clean off any excess flash and mould lines with a needle file and sharp scalpel. I found it easier at this stage to set the horses and crew to one side and focus on the chariot itself. It was fairly straightforward to figure out how the parts fitted together but, before gluing anything in place, I had a 'dry run' to see if anything needed any further cleaning to fit together correctly.

I started by gluing the three sides of the chariot cab to its base, making sure all the corresponding notches on the panels and base matched up and that, once glued into place, the panels were nice and vertical. I then set it aside to dry. Too much manhandling of the chariot before the superglue had completely dried would run the risk of it falling apart and getting into a bit of a mess. It really pays to take your time with these things! While the cab was drying I attached the yoke to the yoke pole, ensuring that from above the yoke ran at right angles across the pole and when viewed from the front it was horizontal. I returned to the chariot cab while the yoke was drying and attached the wheels. The axle fitted snugly into the holes on the hubs of the wheels, sometimes it is necessary to gently file around the circumference of the axle to make it fit. Once again I checked from above, in front and behind to make sure the wheels were fixed at the correct angles.

Finally I attached the yoke pole to the front of the chariot. At this stage I could have attached the crew models to the inside of the chariot cab (some painters like to paint them in situ) but for ease of painting I preferred to work on the chariot and the crew separately, attaching them once the painting was complete.

I then fixed the horses and crew to separate temporary bases for handling while painting. Small scraps of mounting board or plastic board are ideal for this. The chariot was left un-based for now. Then horses, crew and chariot were all undercoated BLACK. Once the undercoat dried I fully painted the underside of the chariot, the yoke, the yoke pole and the insides of each wheel, gently holding the chariot upside down, and then used a tiny amount of glue to attach the chariot right way up to a temporary base.

I prefer to keep the transition from base colours to highlights as subtle as possible, especially over large surfaces like those on the chariot cab. I generally use at least five layers of paint, achieved by mixing extra tones between the three standard tones in each Foundry paint palette. So for instance, after applying the tone from pot 'A' I then mix a tone using paint from pots 'A' and 'B' before applying the tone from pot 'B' and so on. Ultimately it is possible to create a seamless transition from base colour to final highlight using multiple transitional layers. I have found five to seven layers is ideal for my painting style. A good example of this is the Foundry palette EXPERT

FLESH 127, which contains six pots instead of the usual three.

I wanted the sides and floor of the chariot cab to appear clad in animal skins. A little research into Bronze Age chariots revealed two-tone animal skins of darker coloured patches over a slightly off-white background. I used RAWHIDE LIGHT 11C as the base coat for the off-white areas, adding WHITE to this in small increments, the final highlight effectively being WHITE with only a tiny amount of the RAWHIDE LIGHT 11C added. I used a light brown as the off-white base colour instead of the usual ARCTIC GREY 33 because a brown base seemed more appropriate for animal skins. Other light browns that would have worked equally well are: BUFF LIGHT 7C, MOSS LIGHT 29C, DRAB LIGHT 12C, and SPEARSHAFT LIGHT 13C. I decided not to bring the final highlight up to pure WHITE as this does not give such a natural looking finish. The wooden parts were painted with a subtle grained wood effect, built up by painting the base coat as normal and then the successive highlight coats as parallel lines in a loose imitation of wood grain. I tried not to be too precise with these lines, a much better effect was achieved by allowing them to merge, stop and restart, and deviate from being too straight. Keeping the highlight colours fairly close to the base tone worked better as well; the overall effect I wanted was subtlety, not a striped football shirt! The chariot metalwork was then painted using BRONZE BARREL 103.

The finished chariot was set aside and I started painting the horses. Chariot horses stand fairly close together once based and attached to the chariot so I find it easier to paint them on temporary bases first. I used CHESTNUT 53 as the main horse colour to keep them fairly light. I also wanted a very loose skewbald/piebald effect on one of them and so painted its lower back and flanks in an off-white mix, as with the animal skins described above. I kept the horse trappings and reins fairly dark as it contrasted well with the light horse colour and also, I think, gave them a more realistic worn leather look. I wanted to keep the crests on the horses' headdresses in bright colours without them looking too garish or unnatural, so I used ARCTIC GREY 33B instead of WHITE to mix highlights. RAWHIDE LIGHT 11C and BASE SAND LIGHT 10C are also useful for keeping colours (particularly bright ones such as reds and blues) more natural looking as they are highlighted.

With the horses finished I moved on to the crew. Research into Bronze Age clothing and textiles proved extremely useful when making colour decisions for the clothes; I found some truly fantastic colours and pattern designs. Unfortunately the amount of clothing worn by the models did not lend itself to many of the designs I found (I have retained them for use on future models) but the research gave me a useful insight into the colours I could potentially use. I used the standard flesh tone for the humans in the Greek Mythology range; MEDITERRANEAN FLESH 125. I did not want all the armour to be leather or bronze and so painted one of the helmets in BONE YARD 9. Once finished, all the components were allowed to dry before moving onto the next stage.

I gloss varnished all the finished painting at this point,

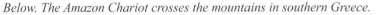

Below. The Amazon Chariot crosses the mountains in southern Greece.

leaving the matt varnish until the whole piece had been constructed. The gloss varnish gave some essential protection to my paintwork while I completed the construction!

I based the finished model on a large MDF base. I did a 'dry run' to check on the best place to attach the horses, which were then glued to the base first. While they were drying I attached the crew to the inside of the chariot cab. As before I did a 'dry run' to make sure both crew would fit comfortably. I could have just glued them, but for added strength I decided to pin one foot of each model to the base of the chariot. Using a pin vice, I drilled a small hole 3-5mm into the foot of the model at its thickest point. Brass wire was then glued into the hole leaving 3-5mm protruding. A corresponding hole was then drilled carefully into the base of the chariot cab and the model securely glued in place.

The whole base was given a covering of modelling putty to hide the integral bases of the horses and provide a level surface for the chariot to sit at the right height. Once this was dry, a pin was carefully inserted into the underside of one of the chariot wheels for fitting into a corresponding hole that I drilled in the base. A small amount of glue was applied to the underside of the yokes and the wheels before finally attaching the chariot. Once dry, the whole base was painted carefully with PVA glue (being careful not to get any on the horses' hooves or the chariot wheels) and dipped into sand. After leaving it to dry again the base was painted, then highlighted by dry brushing, using the BASE SAND 10 palette. I tidied up the base edges with BASE SAND 10B and added static grass and grass clumps as a finishing touch.

Below. The Amazon Chariot.

Chariot Crew	
Skin	MEDITERRANEAN FLESH 125
Hair	CHARCOAL BLACK 34
Armour	BRONZE BARREL 103, RAW-HIDE 11 plus BONE YARD 9, DARK AFRICAN FLESH 121
Leather Goods	TAN 14 plus CHARCOAL BLACK 34 plus ARCTIC GREY 33
Clothes	MADDER RED 60, BRIGHT RED 15, FRENCH BLUE 65, ARCTIC GREY 33
Shoes	RAWHIDE 11
Bow	SPEARSHAFT 13
Horses	
Main Body	CHESTNUT 53, ARCTIC GREY 33, EXPERT FLESH 127
Reins	DARK AFRICAN FLESH 121
Plumes	FRENCH BLUE 65, FRENCH CHASSEUR A CHEVAL GREEN 71, BRONZE BARREL 103, RAWHIDE 11, ARCTIC GREY 33
Chariot	
Wooden Fittings	BAY BROWN 42, SPEARSHAFT 13
Metal Fittings	BRONZE BARREL 103
Main Body and Panels	DEEP BROWN LEATHER 45, RAWHIDE 11, ARCTIC GREY 33

Above. Some Amazons fight in the manner of the City-state Greeks, in close battle order, in striking contrast to the swarms of archers who form the rest of the Amazon battle host.

Below. An Amazon Queen passes a temple of the Gods.

PAINTING THE CYCLOPS
KEVIN DALLIMORE

The Cyclopes were giant men with one eye in the centre of their foreheads. The best known of these creatures is Polyphemus, a son of Poseidon, who held Odysseus and his crew captive in his cave. He ate six of Odysseus' comrades before the hero managed to get him drunk and blind him with a sharpened stake. Polyphemus and his fellow Cyclopes were rough and simple creatures that spent most of their time tending their livestock, but other traditions show the Cyclopes as skilled smiths and artisans. Three of them served Zeus, ruler of the Gods, and built his thunderbolts, while others constructed the walls of great cities like Tiryns and Mycenae, or worked with Hephaestus at his forge in Mount Etna.

Above. Cyclops with COL124 - NORTH AFRICAN FLESH, hair in COL034 - CHARCOAL BLACK and a brown eye in PP042B - BAY BROWN. Animal skin is painted in COL053 - CHESTNUT.

Above. Cyclopes defend the temple.

The Cyclops is one of the iconic images of the Greek myths; an obvious choice of subject for a detailed painting guide for this book. It was also a great opportunity to use the Foundry flesh palettes, which I designed for this sort of occasion; these Cyclopes do have a lot of flesh to cover! The large areas of bare skin means they are otherwise quite simple models, with very little in the way of clothing, weaponry and other gear, so they are a good place to start painting a selection of mythical Greek characters!

For this guide I concentrated on one Cyclops model, using the flesh palette: COL119 - SOUTH AMERICAN FLESH. He was painted in my usual three stage painting technique, which is detailed and explained in great depth in both my Painting Guides (which are also published by

Foundry Publications). Throughout the guide there are also photographs of more Cyclopes that I painted using the other Foundry flesh palettes.

THE EYE OF THE BEHOLDER

I will be going into great depth about painting the Cyclops' eye. Please forgive such a lengthy explanation of a seemingly simple task, but I think the eye is the most important part of this model!

PREPARATION & UNDERCOATING

I began work by using a scalpel to remove all excess metal such as mould lines and flash, scraping the blade

Below. Using a scalpel to remove all excess metal such as mould lines and flash, scraping the blade carefully along the mould line to carve it away before gently tidying and smoothing the area with a fine file.

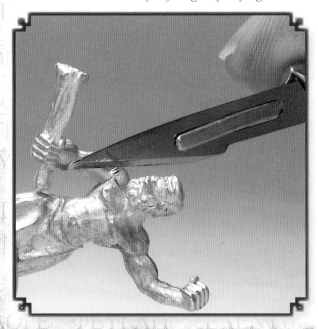

Above. After cleaning up, the Cyclops is attached to a painting stand for convenience during painting.

Above. Cyclops with COL120 - NATIVE AMERICAN FLESH and blue eye in PP020C - DEEP BLUE LIGHT.

carefully along the mould line to carve it away before gently tidying and smoothing the area with a fine file. Please, always be extremely careful when using a sharp knife to do this! This model was well cast and had few mould lines and little flash, but I still checked over it with a critical eye to ensure there were no imperfections, paying particular attention to the large areas of muscle. Any bits of extraneous metal will become all too apparent later if they are not sorted out before painting. There is nothing worse than almost finishing a model before discovering a mould line that cannot be disguised!

After cleaning up, I attached the Cyclops to a painting stand for convenience. Using this I would not have to directly handle, and therefore get finger marks on, the model or inadvertently rub off any paint or undercoat while painting.

UNDERCOAT

The undercoat used was matt black enamel, but PP034A - BLACK would do fine as an alternative. The enamel was thinned by about 10% white spirit and painted on with a large old brush. Always make sure the undercoat is not so thick that it softens the fine details of the model, or so thin that it does not give complete coverage. Once the whole model was coated I put it aside to dry, checking back after ten minutes to make sure the undercoat had not pooled anywhere in big blobs.

Below. Make sure the undercoat is brushed on smoothly; don't allow it to run or pool. Once you have covered the whole model in undercoat put it aside to dry.

Above. The eye is large and well defined on this model, but I still needed very little paint on the brush and it still needed to be a good brush with a good point; PURE SABLE FINE DETAIL and SABLE MIX FINE FINISH.

PAINTING THE EYE!

PICTURE 1: THE WHITES

As the Cyclops only has one eye, I thought it was worth spending some time getting it as good as I could. The first job was to paint in the white with PP033C - WHITE. The eye is large and well defined on this model, which was a great help, but I still needed very little paint on the brush and it still needed to be a good brush with a good point; PURE SABLE FINE DETAIL and SABLE MIX FINE FINISH were my brushes of choice. The paint itself was thinned slightly so that it flowed easily. I tackled the eye first so that if I accidentally painted outside the socket a bit I could tidy it up with PP034A – BLACK. When painting eyes, I try to go for a flattened oval shape. In this instance I followed what was sculpted on the model, and with a bit of neatening up I got the shape I wanted.

PICTURE 2: THE IRIS

I added the iris next, again using a good SABLE MIX FINE FINISH brush. The paint needed to be a bit thicker than for the white because I wanted it to form a tiny blob on the end of the brush hairs, so that when I painted it on, the iris would be circular. A careful aim was needed for this job. It is best to practice on something other then the actual model first. Painting a succession of dots on a piece of scrap card to give an idea of how much paint and how much pressure to use can be helpful. A tiny amount of paint was all that I needed so I was careful not to fill up the brush hair, only dipping the very tip of the brush in the paint. The paint used for this iris was PP042B - BAY BROWN, a slightly lighter brown than I would normally use because I wanted to add a pupil to the eye. This would not be visible if the brown was too dark.

PICTURE 3: THE PUPIL

Admittedly, this final stage of the eye could be omitted for the sake of speed! I have included it in this guide to show how the large eye of the Cyclops provides an opportunity for a little extra detail, and because I just fancied having a go! I needed my best and finest brush for this part, a PURE SABLE FINE DETAIL. The pupil was added in pure black (it being a hole through which light passes) using PP034A - BLACK, thinned a bit from normal. I needed only a minuscule amount of paint on the brush tip to apply a tiny dot in the centre of the iris. I actually hold my breath when performing this kind of very fine detail work. A magnifier could prove handy for doing this. I don't use one (yet) but many painters I know use them and swear by them!

Left. Painting the pupil. Admittedly, this final stage of the eye could be omitted for the sake of speed! I have included it in this guide to show how the large eye of the Cyclops provides an opportunity for a little extra detail, and because I just fancied having a go!

Above. Start by painting around the eyes as this is the hardest bit to do and needs the most care. Then, working away from the eye, fill in the rest of the face. Then do the hands, feet and junctions between the flesh and other objects.

PAINTING THE FLESH SHADE

The large flesh areas on this model were the ideal opportunity to try out COL119 - SOUTH AMERICAN FLESH. COL5 FLESH and the rest of Foundry's flesh palettes would give equally good results.

PICTURE 4

I used PURE SABLE FINE FINISH and PURE SABLE GENERAL DETAIL brushes to cover the flesh areas. I started by painting around the eye as this was the trickiest bit to do. With only a little paint on the brush I carefully painted up to the eye, directing my paint strokes along the eyelids (the top one first) with PP119A - SOUTH AMERICAN FLESH SHADE.

PICTURE 5

Working away from the eye, I then filled in the rest of

Below. The flesh shade coat finished.

the face, gradually putting more paint on the brush at this stage. The hands were next, then the feet, and then the areas where the flesh meets other objects such as the loincloth. The most difficult bits were always painted first, like the fingers and toes.

PICTURE 6

Once all the tricky bits were done I could relax a bit and fill in the rest of the flesh.

Below. Cyclops with COL127 - EXPERT FLESH and blue eye in PP020C - DEEP BLUE LIGHT.

PAINTING THE FLESH MAIN COLOUR

The same principles applied to the next layer of paint; the mid-tone or main colour of the flesh. The only difference here was the need to leave some of the first coat visible as a dark tone in areas that required shade; around the junctions between different colours, in the depressions in the musculature and the lines and creases of the face. As with the shade coat, I did the difficult bits first.

PICTURE 7

With just a little paint on the brush, I carefully added in the top eyelid with PP119B - SOUTH AMERICAN FLESH first. I then painted the rest of the forehead, leaving the shade visible between it and the top eyelid. The rest of the face came next, starting with the bottom eyelid and working down the cheeks and nose. I left the crow's feet, the small creases at the sides of the eye, in the shade colour. The bottom lip was also painted in PP119B - SOUTH AMERICAN FLESH.

PICTURE 8

I dotted in the nipples and then painted around them before filling in the rest of the flesh, leaving the depressions in the musculature in the shade colour. The photographs show how little of the shade layer was left visible.

PAINTING THE FLESH HIGHLIGHT COLOUR

Following on from the flesh mid-tone, I painted in the difficult flesh highlights first.

PICTURE 9

The top eyelid was highlighted with PP119C - SOUTH AMERICAN FLESH LIGHT. Then I painted in the rest of the forehead highlights, leaving the mid-tone and shade showing between it and the top eyelid. Highlights for the rest of the face, the fingers and toes followed. The bottom lip was NOT highlighted. I left it in the darker PP119B - SOUTH AMERICAN FLESH.

PICTURE 10

The highlight was added in the same places as the main mid-tone colour, but leaving some of the mid-tone exposed.

Below. The highlight goes in the same places as the main colour but leaves some of the main colour exposed.

This page. Cyclopes prepare for battle.

Above. The hair shade layer goes all over the mass of hair, the next colours picking up individual strands.

THE OTHER BITS

The rest of the model was finished with similar techniques, so I will limit my explanation of these areas and let the pictures do the talking!

PAINTING THE HAIR

PICTURES 11, 12, 13, 14 & 15

The hair was painted with the three colours of COL057 - STONE. The shade layer was applied all over the mass of hair, with the next two colours picking out individual strands. The final touch was a small dash of white PP033C – WHITE at the temples and chin.

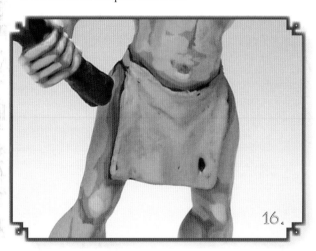

PAINTING THE LOINCLOTH

PICTURES 16, 17 & 18

The loincloth was painted with the three colours of COL007 - BUFF LEATHER. The cloth has some very nice falling folds sculpted on it; making the most of these details with the three stage technique is always a joy!

Left & Below. The loincloth is painted with the three colours of COL007 - BUFF LEATHER.

PAINTING THE CYCLOPS

Above. The outer bark is quite gnarled giving a good surface to detail using SPEARSHAFT. The centre of the club is painted to represent light wood.

PAINTING THE CLUB

PICTURES 19 & 20

The bark of the club was COL013 - SPEARSHAFT with COL009 - BONE YARD for the inner wood. The outer bark is quite gnarled, so it was a good rough surface to detail. I painted the centre of the club very light for contrast, using vague concentric circles to represent the growth rings of the wood from which the club was hewn. And that was it for the painting!

VARNISHING THE MODEL

PICTURES 21 & 22

The Cyclops was left overnight for all the paint to dry thoroughly, and then he was gloss varnished for protection.

Always be careful when applying varnish; if it is too thick it may pool in the recesses of the model. I use an oil based polyurethane gloss varnish as I have not yet found a satisfactory acrylic one.

Once the gloss varnish was dry, I applied a matt varnish. Be even more careful when painting on the matt varnish. It is much better to apply two thin coats than one overly thick one. Brush the varnish out well from any nooks and crannies where it is likely to collect and pool. For matt varnish I now use a soluble artists' varnish. Soluble in this context does not mean it is water soluble; it means it is soluble in white spirit or turpentine. To use, mix up the thick and thin parts of the varnish in the jar according to the maker's instructions for a versatile matt varnish with a slight surface sheen. This is available from good art shops.

Below. Once the gloss varnish was dry, I applied a matt varnish. Be even more careful when painting on the matt varnish. It is much better to apply two thin coats than one overly thick one. Brush the varnish out well from any nooks and crannies where it is likely to collect and pool.

Above. The base on this model is a square plastic base with a sunken recess that the model's metal base drops into. This allows you to build up the filler to the same level as the model's base and so disguise it very successfully.

BASING THE MODEL

PICTURES 23, 24, 25 & 26

I used a square plastic base on this model, with a sunken recess for his metal cast-on base to drop into. I built up the filler to the same level as the model's base to help disguise it successfully. Once it was dry, I coated the surface with sharp sand, left it to dry again, painted it with PP012B - DRAB, left it to dry, and then dry brushed it with PP012C - DRAB LIGHT. I finished off with a light dry brush of

PP009C - BONEYARD LIGHT before applying grass tufts and flock. These were lightly dry brushed with PP004B - OCHRE.

I realise that not everybody uses Foundry paints! I prefer them because I think they are excellent quality and there is a massive selection to choose from, but then I would think that as I helped to create and develop them! The Foundry colour chart at the back of this book should be useful when matching the colours referred to in this article with other paints, and hopefully help to produce a finely painted Cyclops to be proud of!

Below left. The finished model. Below right. Another Cyclops with the same colour flesh.

Above. Miscreants (young Satyrs) have a natural waywardness that serves them well in battle, where they start by hurling empty cups and amphorae at the enemy.

Below. Medusa's horrifying visage turns those who behold it to stone!

Above. The Trojan Hero Hector fights the Chimaera.

Below. Tumbledown shepherd's shack, simple and somewhat run-down in appearance. This is a rural backwater rather than a thriving metropolis.

MAKING RIVERS
MATTHEW FLETCHER

Above. The River.

Above. **Picture One**: *Cut the desired number of sections out of a sheet of hardboard or MDF, each approximately six inches long by four inches across.*

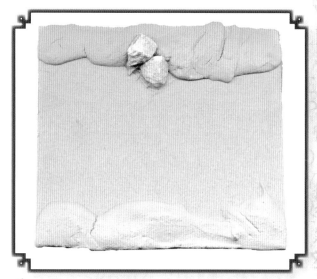

Above. **Picture Two**: *Create the river banks by mixing plaster-based filler with PVA glue, sand, and any old brown paint that you have to hand.*

Rivers and streams appear in more than one of the games in this book (and are essential for keeping your Water Nymphs happy) so here are some fast and cost-effective ideas for how to make them. The sections shown here have been mostly painted blue. This may not be the most true-to-life water colour but it looks more effective on the tabletop than natural browns or greens, and it makes for striking and attractive battlefield scenery.

Picture One: Cut the desired number of sections out of a sheet of hardboard or MDF, each approximately six inches long by four inches across (for illustrative purposes the sections shown here are slightly smaller). It is a good idea to cut out enough sections to stretch the entire length of your gaming table. Remember to include some winding bend sections; feel free to make them as winding and wobbly as you like, but be sure to have both ends of every

single section the same width so that all sections can butt together without overlaps. Now draw a line roughly one centimetre / half an inch in from either edge. Again you must ensure that the ends of each line match up with those on the other sections otherwise your river will not fit together correctly! For each section, chamfer the edges with a sharp blade and sand down, making sure that you make all cuts away from your body as the last thing you want is a Greek tragedy…

Picture Two: Create the river banks by mixing plaster-based filler with PVA glue (this adds strength to the mix), sand, and any old brown paint that you have to hand. The paint is added at this stage so that, should your river sections get chipped during use, any damage is less glaringly obvious and easier to quickly cover up. Your mixture should have a consistency thick enough to

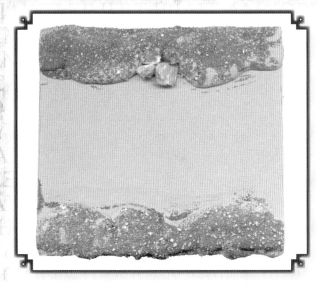

Above. **Picture Three***: Once the mix has hardened, paint the river banks with a mixture of water and PVA glue and sprinkle with sand.*

Above. **Picture Four***: give the banks a good coat of mid-tone brown paint; PP013B - SPEARSHAFT is ideal.*

hold its shape without running everywhere or, at the other extreme, being too dense to spread. It may take a little trial and error to get the consistency right. If it seems a bit too runny, leave it to thicken slightly for a few minutes. Once the mixture is ready, daub it onto your pencilled bank sections so that it creates a slight slope. The exact shape and gradient of the banks is down to personal preference, as are any additional small stones, twig-debris or similar items embedded in the bank for decoration.

Picture Three: Once the mix has hardened, paint the river banks with a mixture of 50/50 water and PVA glue and sprinkle with sand, making sure you get complete coverage (this is the same technique that you would use to base a model).

Picture Four: Leave your river sections overnight to give the wet sand time to dry and set in place properly. Then give the banks a good coat of mid-tone brown paint; PP013B - SPEARSHAFT is ideal. You can make as much mess as you like at this stage, you can tidy it up when you paint the river itself later.

Below. **Picture Five***: When the brown banks have dried, apply a good solid dry brush of a suitable highlight.*

Picture Five: When the brown banks have dried, apply a good solid dry brush of a suitable highlight; COL010 - BASE SAND (all three tones; A, B and C) was used here. A good tip when basing / painting a larger area of terrain in this way is to go over the top of this with a further dry brush of a *yellowy* colour like PP004B - OCHRE, then a final light brush of PP010C - BASE SAND LIGHT to finish off. The point of this is to give the dry brushing some depth and prevent the painted sections from looking washed out and pastelly.

Picture Six: IMPORTANT, READ THIS WHOLE SECTION BEFORE BEGINNING! With the banks finished, the water itself now needs painting. Use a dark blue (PP066B -PRUSSIAN BLUE does the job nicely) for the first coat. Once this has had a chance to dry, slap on a thick coat of the same colour and, while it is still wet, paint a broad stripe of dark green or black straight down the centre, and a highlight of sky blue along the edges. It might appear as if you have completely ruined your river sections at this stage, but there is method to this madness! While the whole mess of paints is still wet,

Below. **Picture Six***: With the banks finished, the water itself now needs painting. Use a dark blue for the first coat.*

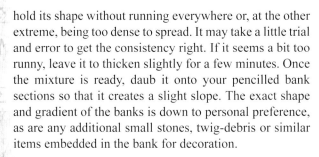

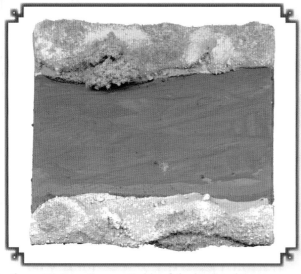

Above. **Picture Seven**: *To blend the banks of the river into your gaming board, stick small patches of flock to them using a 50/50 water and PVA mix.*

deep water towards the centre. If this technique sounds intimidating, or you are concerned about it going wrong, you can just paint your river sections blue, but the above method is strongly recommended. It is nowhere near as difficult as it sounds and it will give you a great effect!

Picture Seven: To blend the banks of the river into your gaming board, stick small patches of flock to them using a 50/50 water and PVA mix. You might also want to add reeds (cut from old paint brushes or brooms), foliage clumps, flotsam and jetsam, or whatever else fits the look of your gaming table.

Picture Eight: Now varnish your river sections. Make sure at this stage that the individual sections are not sat on a surface that could be damaged by puddles of varnish, or situated in a confined space. Inhalation of fumes and ruining the kitchen table can be equally hazardous to your health! While it is possible to purchase all manner of expensive professional water effects, cheap yacht varnish (available from any good DIY store) can literally be poured to a couple of millimetres' depth onto the water parts of each section and spread with a brush to achieve just as nice a result. Be aware that this may take several days to dry if applied thickly, but you should find it provides you with a natural ripple effect on the surface that is well worth the wait!

use a thinly watered down wash of your original blue to blend along the borders between the different stripes of colour. The overall effect you are going for is to merge the different colours together, starting light at the edges and growing darker towards the middle. This should give a representation of shallow water along the banks and

Above. **Picture Eight**: *Now varnish your river sections. Make sure at this stage that the individual sections are not sat on a surface that could be damaged by puddles of varnish, or situated in a confined space. Inhalation of fumes and ruining the kitchen table can be equally hazardous to your health!*

Below. The river flowing to a ford.

Above. An example of several river sections placed together.

Below. An example of using brown paints instead of blue to create a stagnant water feature.

Above. City-states Hoplites are armed with a round shield, called a hoplon, which covers them from neck to knee. With a helmet, cuirass and greaves as well, and fighting in a close formation, they offer few gaps for enemy weapons.

Below. Warriors sprout from a dragon's teeth sown by King Aeetes.

THE FOUNDRY PAINT SYSTEM

The Foundry Paint System has warm, glowing colours with real depth, just like the ones we've been mixing ourselves for years. Each pot has 20ml of paint with lids that really provide an airtight seal so your paint will stay usable for ages. In the Foundry Paint System each main colour is teamed up with the highlight and shading colours, so that you can quickly achieve results like those you see on our web site **www.wargamesfoundry.com**, in our adverts and, of course, on the painted models in this book.

SHADE 1A	LEMON 1B	LIGHT 1C	SHADE 20A	DEEP BLUE 20B	LIGHT 20C	SHADE 42A	BAY BROWN 42B	LIGHT 42C
SHADE 2A	YELLOW 2B	LIGHT 2C	SHADE 21A	SKY BLUE 21B	LIGHT 21C	SHADE 44A	BURNING GOLD 44B	LIGHT 44C
SHADE 3A	ORANGE 3B	LIGHT 3C	SHADE 22A	VIVID BLUE 22B	LIGHT 22C	SHADE 45A	DEEP BROWN LEATHER 45B	LIGHT 45C
SHADE 4A	OCHRE 4B	LIGHT 4C	SHADE 23A	TOMB BLUE 23B	LIGHT 23C	SHADE 53A	CHESTNUT 53B	LIGHT 53C
SHADE 5A	FLESH 5B	LIGHT 5C	SHADE 24A	TEAL BLUE 24B	LIGHT 24C	SHADE 54A	CONKER BROWN 54B	LIGHT 54C
SHADE 6A	DUSKY FLESH 6B	LIGHT 6C	SHADE 25A	BRIGHT GREEN 25B	LIGHT 25C	SHADE 55A	BUTTER FUDGE 55B	LIGHT 55C
SHADE 7A	BUFF LEATHER 7B	LIGHT 7C	SHADE 26A	FOREST GREEN 26B	LIGHT 26C	SHADE 56A	PALOMINO 56B	LIGHT 56C
SHADE 8A	CANVAS 8B	LIGHT 8C	SHADE 27A	STORM GREEN 27B	LIGHT 27C	SHADE 57A	STONE 57B	LIGHT 57C
SHADE 9A	BONE YARD 9B	LIGHT 9C	SHADE 28A	PHLEGM GREEN 28B	LIGHT 28C	SHADE 65A	FRENCH BLUE 65B	LIGHT 65C
SHADE 10A	BASE SAND 10B	LIGHT 11C	SHADE 29A	MOSS 29B	LIGHT 29C	SHADE 67A	AUSTRIAN WHITE 67B	LIGHT 67C
SHADE 11A	RAWHIDE 11B	LIGHT 11C	SHADE 30A	RAW LINEN 30B	LIGHT 30C	SHADE 68A	BRITISH REDCOAT 68B	LIGHT 68C
SHADE 12A	DRAB 12B	LIGHT 12C	SHADE 31A	GRANITE 31B	LIGHT 31C	SHADE 70A	FRENCH DRAGOON GREEN 70B	LIGHT 70C
SHADE 13A	SPEARSHAFT 13B	LIGHT 13C	SHADE 32A	SLATE GREY 32B	LIGHT 32C	SHADE 72A	MUSKET STOCK BROWN 72B	LIGHT 72C
SHADE 14A	TAN 14B	LIGHT 14C	SHADE 33A	ARCTIC GREY 33B	WHITE 33C	SHADE 104A	GUN METAL 104B	LIGHT 104C
SHADE 15A	BRIGHT RED 15B	LIGHT 15C	BLACK 34A	CHARCOAL BLACK 34B	LIGHT 34C	SHADE 108A	BRITISH GUN GREY 108B	LIGHT 108C
SHADE 16A	NIPPLE PINK 16B	LIGHT 16C	SHADE 37A	TERRACOTTA 37B	LIGHT 37C	SHADE 119A	SOUTH AMERICAN FLESH 119B	LIGHT 119C
SHADE 17A	WINE STAIN RED 17B	LIGHT 17C	SHADE 38A	SCARLET 38B	LIGHT 38C	SHADE 125A	MEDITER-RANEAN FLESH 125B	LIGHT 125C
SHADE 19A	ROYAL PURPLE 19B	LIGHT 19C	SHADE 39A	STORM BLUE 39B	LIGHT 39C	SHADE 126A	AFRICAN FLESH 126B	LIGHT 126C

Kevin Dallimore's Painting & Modelling Guide
MASTER CLASS

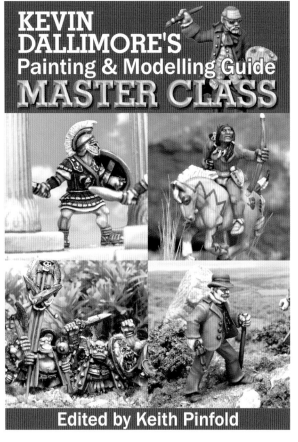

KEVIN DALLIMORE'S Painting & Modelling Guide MASTER CLASS

Edited by Keith Pinfold

Everything you ever wanted to know about painting miniatures and models to a professional standard is contained in this 308 page book.

Kevin Dallimore and over twenty five other renowned and respected painters and modellers reveal the techniques they use to give their miniatures and models that great professional finish; techniques such as varnishing, dry brushing, non metallic metal, shading, highlighting, blending, textured leather and the use of diluted washes are all discussed in depth together with many modelling ideas too; ideas for doing conversions, creating dioramas, making and painting scenery, vehicles and many more. All of the processes described in the many different articles are fully detailed and coupled with photographs of each important stage.

Initially, Kevin goes quickly through the all important basics before clearly detailing all of the advanced techniques that he and his fellow painters use to produce great looking models. There then follow many articles where guest painters and modellers share their thoughts and ideas on particular techniques when painting historical, fantasy and sci-fi models: Old West, Napoleonic, Ancients, Romans, Swashbucklers, WW2, Goblins, Orcs, Beastmen, Trolls, Judge Dredd and lots more.

By copying the methods and techniques in this book and with a little determination and practice, everyone will be able to produce painted miniatures and models to a standard that previously they had only dreamed of.

FOREWORD

THE THREE COLOUR METHOD

MODELLING INTERLUDE PART 1 VEHICLES

PAINTING: THAT PROFESSIONAL TOUCH

STEP 5 THE BASE

ORCS, ORCS, ORCS!
Paul Baker

FLESH RECIPES

PAINTING NAPOLEON CROSSING THE ALPS
Sascha Herm

KEVIN DALLIMORE'S ORIGINAL GUIDE TO PAINTING AND BUILDING MINIATURE MODELS

If you're entirely new to painting then this guide will help to get you started, and if you have painted before you'll find it full of useful tips and new ideas.

With the aid of fully illustrated stage-by-stage examples Kevin describes every aspect of his celebrated painting style, with a quick and simple method designed to get you painting single models and armies to a high standard.

Many areas of miniature model painting are examined in detail, with sections covering the equipment you'll need, the preparation of models, designing and painting shields, using transfers, painting horses using oils, varnishing and basing. There are also hints and tips from some well-known guest painters.

Illustrated throughout with a vast number of painted examples featuring Kevin's stunning work, this guide should inspire miniature model enthusiasts everywhere to pick up those paint brushes!

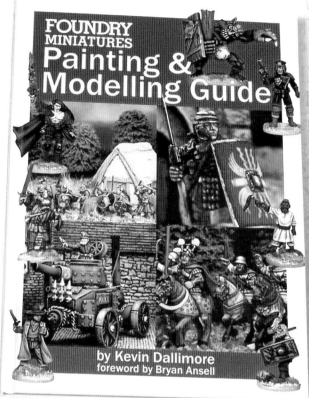

FOUNDRY MINIATURES Painting & Modelling Guide

by Kevin Dallimore
foreword by Bryan Ansell

"If you paint wargames scale model soldiers you need to read this book"

Chris Steadman

"Looks fantastic. Full-colour Eye Candy everywhere you look"

Steve Dean

BULL RUN TO GETTYSBURG

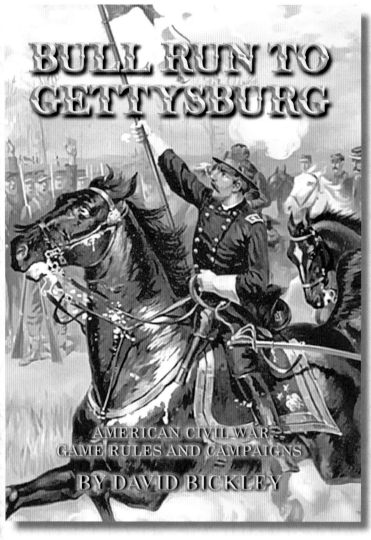

AMERICAN CIVIL WAR GAME RULES AND CAMPAIGNS

BY DAVID BICKLEY

As a defining moment in United States history, the American Civil War has no equal, which is why it remains such a fascinating subject even today.

If you are interested in painting, collecting or gaming with model soldiers, or interested in the American Civil War in any way then this book is for you.

As well as many articles that set the scene and atmosphere of the period, this book contains painting guides, game rules and campaigns that are informative and great fun to play.

This full colour book, lavishly illustrated with stunning photography of lots of magnificently painted miniatures is all you need to recreate the battles and tactics of the American Civil War. .

A4 Hardback, 176 pages, lavishly illustrated in full colour throughout

CENTRAL AFRICA
ARMIES OF THE NINETEENTH CENTURY: AFRICA
by Chris Peers Drawings by Ian Heath

This is the second volume in Foundry's projected series describing the armies of the era of exploration in sub-Saharan Africa. Following a similar format to its predecessor, it covers the area now largely occupied by the countries of Gabon, the Republic of Congo (Brazzaville), the Democratic Republic of Congo, Rwanda, Burundi, Zambia, and Malawi. This was the archetypal 'Darkest Africa' of 19th-century exploration, and many of its indigenous inhabitants lived at the time in remote regions. Consequently most of what we know about these peoples comes from the fleeting impressions of such European travellers as encountered them – and all too often their experiences were limited to a flight of arrows from an unseen enemy concealed in the forest. This book therefore sets out put such confrontations into context, and to describe the organisation, tactics, costumes and weapons of the protagonists in this unique theatre of conflict.

A4 sized hardback with traditional linen and glittering gilt binding, 152 pages. Chris Peers' authoritative text is accompanied by 120 drawings of warriors, troop types and flags, 61 illustrations, 3 maps.

JAPAN AND KOREA
ARMIES OF THE NINETEENTH CENTURY: ASIA
Written and Illustrated by Ian Heath

This volume provides a detailed study of the astonishing reinvention of the Empire of Japan during the 19th century as it emerged from 200 years of self-imposed isolation to become a military superpower. As late as the 1850s the country remained technologically and militarily stagnant, but within just 40 years – in what must rank as the most rapid and comprehensive cultural transformation in world history – it had managed not only to absorb and successfully imitate several hundred years of Western technological progress, but had become one of the late Victorian world's top ten military powers. During the same timeframe it also embraced the concept of colonialism, and with its invasion of China in 1894 and virtual occupation of Korea soon after took its first fateful steps along a road that would lead, with horrible inevitability, to head-on collision with the Allies in World War Two. The evolution of its army, arms, uniforms and tactics during the 19th century are all covered, from samurai armour to Western uniforms, and from katana to Krupps. Korea, by contrast, participated only reluctantly in military modernisation, and adopted a limited programme of reform only under foreign pressure – especially Japanese, but also American, Russian and Chinese – in the closing decades of the century. Such reforms as the country attempted nevertheless proved too little and too late, and were insufficient to prevent Korea becoming first a puppet state and then a colony of its maritime neighbour. The final part of the book comprises a detailed index for the five volumes of the series published thus far.

A4 sized hardback with traditional linen and glittering gilt binding, 172 pages. Illustrations include 133 figures, 57 illustrations and maps.

INDIA'S NORTH-EAST FRONTIER

The Abors, the Akas, Assam, Cachar, the Chin-Lushai, the Daflas, the Garos, the Khamtis, the Khasis, Manipur, the Mikirs, the Mishmis, the Nagas, the Singphos and Tripura. First ever in-depth study of a neglected theatre of British colonial conflict. This is the first ever in-depth study of one of the most remote and neglected theatres of 19th-century colonial conflict, where for decades British and Indian troops fought a forgotten war against merciless warbands of head-hunters and slave-raiders. A4 sized hardback with traditional linen and glittering gilt binding, 192 pages. Illustrations include 125 figures, 53 other illustrations and nine maps.

THE AZTEC & INCA EMPIRES,
OTHER NATIVE PEOPLES OF THE AMERICAS,
THE CONQUISTADORES

The Caribbean 1492-1603, Mesoamerica c.1450-1600, South America 1500-1600, North America 1497-1608, Spanish America 1492-1600. This book provides a detailed examination of the Aztec, Inca, and other native armies of North, Central, and South America from the mid-15th century to the early 17th, and of the European explorers and invaders with whom they came into conflict. There are details of the arms, dress, organisation, and tactics of the principal peoples of each region. Includes 247 drawings of warriors and soldiers taken from contemporary pictures or reconstructed from eyewitness descriptions.

THE FOUNDRY COMPENDIUM
PIRATES TO DARKEST AFRICA

The Foundry Compendium is packed with rules, painting advice and ideas for making great-looking terrain. It will appeal to anyone interested in playing games such as exploration in Darkest Africa, fighting for survival and glory in Rome's gladiatorial arenas and plundering the West African coast with your band of cutthroat pirates. Themed to concentrate on Pirates and Darkest Africa, but covering other historical periods too; Aztecs, Gladiators, Greeks and Romans. 96 pages, lavishly illustrated in full colour throughout. A4 Softback.

THE RULES WITH NO NAME
RULES FOR THE OLD WEST

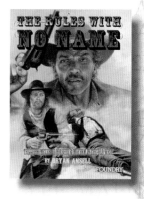

The Rules With No Name are a straightforward set of rules for gunfights in the age of the Cowboy and the Indian, the Lawman and the Outlaw. Classic encounters are played out using 28mm miniatures in an easy-to-learn game full of subtle complexity. The innovative Fate Deck introduces a fun and realistic element of chance while simple rules for movement, shooting and fighting allow for quick, friendly games in which players will find themselves presented with a deceptively challenging set of tactical choices from one turn to the next. This book contains all the rules you will need to play. 136 pages, lavishly illustrated in full colour throughout.

THE PARAGUAYAN WAR
ORGANISATION, WARFARE, DRESS AND WEAPONS

The Paraguayan War, sometimes referred to as the Triple Alliance War, was a sanguinary conflict of attrition fought mostly within a triangle of land formed by the Parana, Terry Hooker provides not only a lucid account of the war itself – the largest ever fought in South America – but also an outline of the convoluted political and military events which led up to it. 192 pages. Illustrations include 252 figures, 60 illustrations, 16 maps.

Just one of a long series of definitive military reference books, with volumes covering the armies of a variety of periods and nations, mostly presented in an A4 sized hardback format with traditional linen and glittering gilt binding.

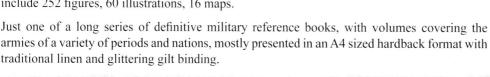

RIVALS OF THE RAJ
NON-BRITISH COLONIAL ARMIES IN ASIA 1497–1941

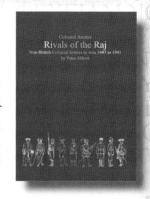

This volume features the armies of the Austro-Hungarian Empire, Denmark, The Netherlands, France, Germany, Portugal, Spain, America, Belgium, Italy and Sweden!Covering those Asian armies which fought alongside the British, from the foundations laid in 1497 to the demise of company rule. This book examines in detail the developments in the structure, armament, and uniforms of the armies maintained by the imperial powers in Asia throughout the colonial period. A4 sized hardback with traditional linen and glittering gilt binding, 192 pages. Illustrations include 243 figures, 53 other illustrations and 4 maps.

RISINGS AND REBELLIONS 1919-39
INTERWAR COLONIAL CAMPAIGNS IN AFRICA, ASIA AND THE AMERICAS

Following on from the author's highly-acclaimed Small Wars and Skirmishes, this volume covers the most significant 'small wars' of the interwar period up to the Italian occupation of Abyssinia in 1935–36. The author illustrates the main types of campaign involved, the organisation of forces, the effects of new weaponry, and the tactics that the indigenous peoples adopted to counter the technology of the colonial invaders. A4 sized hardback with traditional linen and glittering gilt binding, 192 pages. Illustrations include 137 drawings of soldiers, 50 other illustrations and maps.

BURMA AND INDO-CHINA
THE KINGDOM OF AVA, THE KACHINS, THE KARENS, THE SHAN STATES, THE WA. CAMBODIA, THE LAO STATES, SIAM & VIETNAM

This volume covers a region which witnessed fierce competition between Britain and France during the 19th century, as each sought to establish a southern trade route into China while at the same time continuing the vigorous jockeying for local political pre-eminence. A4 sized hardback with traditional linen and glittering gilt binding. 207 pages, over 60 pictures and maps, over 160 line illustrations.

THE AFRICAN KNIGHTS
ARMIES OF THE 19TH CENTURY EASTERN AFRICAN SAVANNAH

The Armies of Sokoto, Bornu and Bagirmi in the Nineteenth Century. This book provides a description of what was, in the 19th century, one of the most neglected parts of the African continent, but was at the same time, without doubt, one of the most culturally sophisticated — the eastern Savannah, an area now divided between the modern countries of Nigeria, Niger, Mali, and Cameroon. It begins with the Sokoto jihad and ends with the conquest of the Savannah states by Europeans. A4 softback with colour covers, 64 pages illustrated throughout with black and white contemporary photographs and engravings.

CHINA
19TH CENTURY IMPERIAL CHINA

The Celestial Empire's traditional distrust of all foreigners, exacerbated by misunderstandings guaranteed that relations between the Empire and the Western world would lead to war. This book is an illustrated study of the Empire's armed forces during this turbulent period, its organisational structure, arms, uniforms, and tactics. Such foreign-officered units as the Ever-Victorious Army are also covered, as are the armies of the many revolutionary movements, including the Taipings, Boxers, Panthays, Miao, Tungans, and Nien. A4 sized hardback with traditional linen and glittering gilt binding. 174 pages, illustrations include 183 drawings of warriors and soldiers, 39 other illustrations, and six maps.

FOUNDRY PUBLICATIONS

GOD OF BATTLES

LOW CUNNING & BLOODY COMBAT IN AN AGE OF WARRING GODS

A TABLETOP BATTLE GAME

By Jake Thornton

MAGIC,
MYTH &
MAYHEM
FANTASY GAMING
RULES
LIKE YOU HAVE
NEVER SEEN BEFORE!

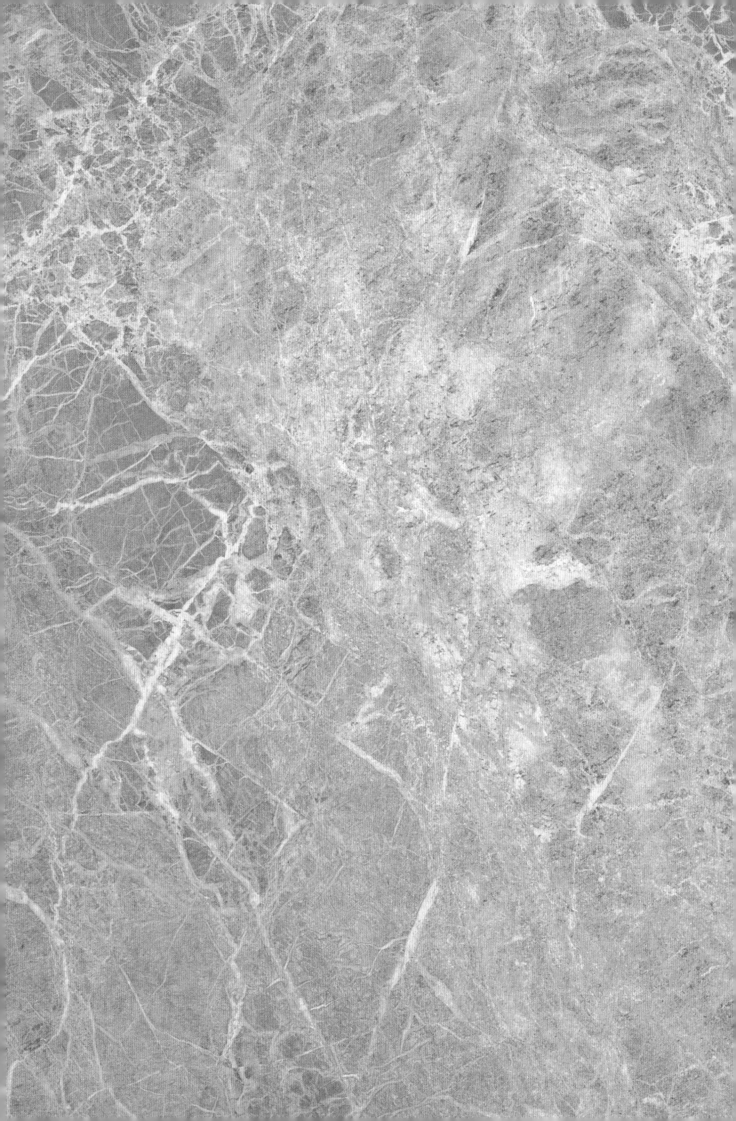